BILL WI

# STRAINING AT THE OARS

## [ ENCOUNTERING JESUS IN THE STORMS OF LIFE ]

Ark House Press
arkhousepress.com

Cataloguing in Publication Data:
Title: Straining At the Oars
ISBN: 978-0-6454117-8-2 (pbk)
Subjects: REL012040 [RELIGION / Christian Living / Inspirational]; REL023000 [RELIGION / Christian Ministry / Discipleship]; REL012120 [RELIGION / Christian Living / Spiritual Growth]

Design by initiateagency.com

"Immediately Jesus made his disciples get into the boat and go on ahead of him to Bethsaida, while he dismissed the crowd. After leaving them, he went up on a mountainside to pray. Later that night, the boat was in the middle of the lake, and he was alone on land. He saw the disciples **straining at the oars**, because the wind was against them."[1]

"Be merciful to me, O God, be merciful to me, for in you my soul takes refuge; in the shadow of your wings I will take refuge, till the **storms of destruction** pass by."[2]

---

[1]    Mark 6.45-48a, NIV
[2]    Psalm 57.1, ESV

# CONTENTS

# ABOUT THE AUTHOR

I f you are reading this book, you probably do so because of your relationship with me. Or, you may have been given this book by someone who knows me. It could be you are reading it out of curiosity. No matter the reason, allow me to share a little about who I am and how this book came about.

This book is partly the result of realizing that throughout 60-plus years of life, I have been *straining at the oars*. I have worn various hats for my entire life, including ones I probably didn't even realize I was wearing at the time. These hats are son, brother, friend, student, husband, father, son-in-law, father-in-law, pastor, employee, boss, classmate, teammate, roommate, neighbor, stranger, chaplain, cheerleader (not literally), comforter, companion, coach, and mentor, as well as other has I may not have even been aware of wearing. These hats have become weather-beaten, battered, worn out, and even thrown away.

The one hat I have worn most of my life that will never be thrown away, though it has become weathered and beaten over time, is that of being a follower of Christ. It's not so much a hat that I wear but an identity I proudly claim as a child of God. I have not always lived up to that identity and have, at times, struggled with it. In some of the most difficult times of my life, I have clung to that identity, gripping to the only hope I have in this often chaotic and painful world. Only by God's grace have I been able to endure and persevere through the storms of life that have come my way.

The concept of *straining at the oars* describes the struggles of navigating the storms of life on my own. As someone who aims to please people, I have often been *straining at the oars* to keep everyone happy, including God. In striving to be a *good Christian*, I have found myself *straining at the oars* as if being a *good*, even *perfect*, or *righteous* Christian was how I could please God and others.

Although I take pride in extending grace to everyone, it is most difficult to extend grace to myself. I have struggled to navigate the storms of life that have been exacerbated by trying to do it all in my own strength. The counsel I give to others is not always something I have practiced. The words of wisdom I give to others do not always apply to me. As a pastor for 35 years, I have come alongside people going through a crisis, battling their storms of life, and struggling with what they are supposed to do. I have a great passion for helping people encounter Christ in their storms of life. I have often wondered why I cannot do the same for myself.

Fortunately, God's grace has been sufficient for me in very painful seasons of life. Sometimes the grace of God shows up by an overwhelming sense of God's presence through the Holy Spirit or while reading Scriptures, spending time in prayer, and even in times of silence. There are times when the grace of God shows up in a song, while visiting with a friend, or through the beauty of God's creation. No matter what I am going through, God continues to show up.

The grace of God has shown up for me through a variety of people. Through a friend I have known for over 40 years—thanks, Dupe—and people I have only recently come to know—thanks, Stolzie, Tom, Donnie, Roz and John, as well as through the person God used to help me trust and believe that I had something to offer people with this book—thanks,

Andrew. I have learned that by having a Godly community of people, God can and will produce life out of what appears to be a storm of destruction. Throughout many storms in my life, the grace of God has been more than sufficient for me.

As you read this book, my hope and prayers are that the grace of God will show up for you as you personally encounter Jesus in whatever storms you are in, or that may come your way; that through the Holy Spirit, the grace of God may become more than sufficient for you. I also pray that God will send you people who will help carry you through the storms as He did for me. Or, perhaps this book will be used by you to help carry someone else so they too can encounter Jesus Christ and experience the grace of God no matter what storms they are going through.

Hopefully anyone who reads this book will begin the process I have begun by releasing whatever oars are weighing them down, preventing them from experiencing the abundant life of Christ in this world. It truly is an ongoing process as God brings beauty out of ashes, no matter how those ashes may continue to smolder. My prayer is that a fresh encounter with the grace of God will release the streams of living water given through the outpouring of the Holy Spirit.

# BLESSING

I was fortunate to meet Bill Williamson in 2019 when I was invited to speak to a group of men at the church he was pastoring in Washington State. We connected immediately, and he told me he had a strong feeling God wanted him to write a book. It is the book you are currently reading. I am grateful to have had the chance to mentor him through his writing journey. At that time, neither Bill nor I had any idea about the storm he was about to go through in his life or the one the world was about to experience. In fact, he found out firsthand how appropriate the title *Straining at the Oars* was. God knew and had a plan to help him write an incredible book.

As he strained at his own oars since our meeting in 2019, he was able to write a book with authenticity, passion, and one that honors God. *Straining at the Oars* is an essential guide to help you embrace the storms of life and come through, with the glory of God, to find your purpose in life. I am grateful to have been on this journey with Bill, and I am glad to be able to write this short recommendation. Enjoy the journey you go on as you learn how to keep moving through the storms of life to wonderful triumph on the other side.

Andrew Jobling
andrewjobling.com.au
As seen on Channel 7 Sunrise (https://youtu.be/JDpu6i7QUhc)

# FOREWORD

Life is full of ups and downs. Everyone has seasons of calm and seasons of a storm. When surrounded by people at a restaurant, a ballgame, or a church, you know that everyone has a story. It is likely everyone is in the middle of hardship, has worked through a tribulation, or is heading down the path of an unforeseeable challenge ahead. Life is a storm, and we don't like being driven and tossed by the wind. We don't want our plans to be altered, and we don't want to be slowed by the winds of adversity. One solution is to row harder, paddle faster, and strain at the oars to the point of despair. This is the premise that Pastor Bill Williamson builds on throughout his book. *Straining at the Oars* is a perfect visual aid that encapsulates the struggle we all face.

As you will discover, Bill is well acquainted with storms in his life. Having known each other for over 40 years, I've worked side-by-side with this man of God as he persevered through a master's program at Fuller Theological Seminary while leading a middle school ministry at Ronald Reagan's home megachurch in Bel Air. We've stayed in close contact as he served throughout the different churches and have always found ways to connect on retreats in different parts of the country. As a pastor myself, I can understand and relate to all the storms he has struggled through. *It takes one to know one* is an old catchphrase that is as true of pastors as anything. Bill has learned how to be a good pastor, remain positive, and keep going even through the roughest storms of his life.

Although Bill has been a pastor throughout his adult life, what he shares in the book comes from being a human. Although definitely helpful for pastors, the message of this book is something we all need to have in our lives. Bill has learned many lessons, but he is also gifted at applying them to his own life and sharing them with others. Like Bill, I worked at some very large churches, planted a church, and navigated through the challenges pastors face. He was always quick to listen, encourage and build up when I was down. Bill had the faith and wisdom to open up about his struggles and gather advice when he was down. The lessons he shares in *Straining at the Oars* are not mere truisms Bill picked up in his theological training but principles grounded in Scripture as grounded in his experience.

The message of the book is simple but nuanced. The message isn't to strain harder at the oars when storms come. This is often the world's humanistic message or our own prideful nature. But neither is the book's message to just permanently stop rowing either. Rowing is the ordinary means of progress when going from one side of the Sea of Galilee to the other. Rowing is a good metaphor for the regular rhythms of life. When storms come, it's not enough just to strain harder at the oars. We need help. We need one another. In the Bible, in the book of Galatians, we are told to do our part; in a sense, *to keep up our daily rowing routine.* But in the same chapter, we are told to come to the aid of others when they are burdened by the inevitable storms of life.

*Carry each other's burdens, and in this way you will fulfill the law of Christ,*[3] *for each one should carry their own load.*[4]

---

[3]    Galatians 6:2, NIV
[4]    Galatians 6:5, NIV

In addition to our own rowing and the help of others, we are to rely on the Lord's help. We need the Lord's strength to give us the emotional perseverance necessary. Jesus said, "I am the vine; you are the branches. If you remain in me and I in you, you will bear much fruit; apart from me you can do nothing."[5] These biblical messages have proved to be true for Bill in his life, and I can heartily vouch for them as a soon-to-be-retired pastor of 40 years. Rediscover these truths about when to row, when to strain and when *not* to row as Bill applies them to everyday life. Jesus has promised abundant life to all who follow after him, all who do things his way and take his yoke upon themselves instead of doing things the world's way. Jesus said, "The thief comes only to steal and kill and destroy; I have come that they may have life and have it to the full."[6]

This book is for you if you have been *straining at the oars* too often and too long. Read it, apply it, and find that you can get to the other side of the lake before you know it.

**Paul Duppenthaler BA, MDiv, DMin**
*Planted the Countryside Community Church in Sherwood, Oregon, and is still there (1993)*
*Climbed Mount Kilimanjaro, Tanzania (2017) An avid road cyclist, about 4000 miles a year.*

---

5     John 15:5, NIV
6     John 10:10, NIV

# INTRODUCTION

The idea of *straining at the oars* has been with me for several years. It comes from Mark 6, a time when Jesus sees the disciples on the lake, rowing in their boat when a storm appears. They are *straining at the oars*. Or, as the ESV says, they were *making headway painfully.* I will explain more about that later.

As I thought about *straining at the oars*, I could not help but think about what our world experienced in 2020 at the beginning of the COVID-19 pandemic. Nobody knew what was happening and what the future held as we made our way through the storm. Most people began to realize that life would never go back to *normal*. It was time for everyone to take a deep breath and look for what God was doing, and how *he* would use all things to bring about an even greater purpose in our lives—a new normal. Ultimately, that is what this book is about.

Whatever storms we face, whatever pandemics we find ourselves in, life may go on back normal. Whatever storms continue to mount up against us, we cannot muscle up and go full steam ahead. There comes a time when the best thing to do—the only thing to do—is to stop rowing, stop straining, set down the oars, and prepare for a fresh encounter with God—the Father, Son, and Holy Spirit. God can, and will, give us what we need to not only survive the storms we encounter, but He will get us to the "other shore", the promised land, either here or in eternity.

In the beginning, it wasn't clear what the COVID-19 virus was all about. Nobody knew how it would impact our world, let alone our individual lives. Slowly, like a swell out in the ocean, it began to pick up momentum until it seemed like a tsunami was about to wreak havoc. *Still, really?* We've experienced other viruses and diseases. Surely this virus was not going to be any different. With the little bit of body surfing I did as a teenager, I know that some swells out in the ocean can turn into nothing. You're waiting and waiting for that perfect wave. You see a swell, position yourself, the wave begins to form, then it flattens out. As I watched the swelling of this *novel virus*, I didn't think anything was going to come of it.

There were rumblings about a sickness sweeping China. It was not a threat to America. There were a few reports of the virus making its way to Italy. Still, nothing to worry about here. Unfortunately, this virus made its way across the Atlantic Ocean and eventually crossed our continent, and landed in Seattle, Washington—my state. Still, that was a two-hour drive from Yakima, where I lived at the time.

However, there was a shift in the atmosphere. People in Yakima were glued to the news, hearing about tragic deaths in a nursing home. Then, sure enough, the virus made its way to Yakima. Before anyone knew it, Yakima was on the national news. We were considered a *hot spot*. Yakima was having significant increases in positive cases as well as deaths. We were in *lockdown*, and most people were not allowed to leave their homes.

I remember being in a staff meeting at the church on March 10, 2020. We were *social distancing*, although not wearing masks—yet. I could tell some of the staff were concerned, even slightly frightened. So, I gave them the choice of working from home. I believed it may be two weeks, and all would be good. Later that week, I with some other pastors. We were talking about how some churches all over were canceling worship services. None of us felt our churches were at that point and probably never would be. Yet, that afternoon we canceled our upcoming worship services, as did pastors in other churches. Again, I honestly believed that it would be two weeks and that we would be back doing worship by Easter. Easter came and went, as did many other Sundays. We quickly learned how to record the worship service remotely—everyone involved in the worship service would record their part from home. I spent many days and hours recording sermons from my home. It was frustrating when a 30-minute sermon took several takes. I would end up spending two hours just recording one sermon.

Life as we knew it had changed. The little I did outdoors, like going to the grocery store and taking a walk around the neighborhood, felt like I was living in a ghost town. Amid this sweeping pandemic, there was an increase in fear and panic. It was like *Black Friday*, the shopping extravaganza the day after Thanksgiving when people in America frantically bombard stores offering incredibly ridiculous discounts on hot ticket items. At the beginning of the COVID-19 pandemic, people were racing to the grocery stores and fighting for the last roll of toilet paper on the shelf. There was a run on simple necessities like hand sanitizers, wipes, milk, eggs, water, and flour.

It was not such a short period as I had imagined it would be. Perhaps even as you read this book, the pandemic, or at least COVID-19, is still lingering. The messages being given at the time, like *stay at home, save lives, social distance, and mask up,* created external panic and inner turmoil. Restaurants were ordered to close, and professional sporting events were canceled. It seemed like we were living in some horror movie. Everything was changing. The waters were rising, the waves were crashing down, and those I served with at church wondered what we were going *to do. How were we going to* do *church moving forward?* It was as if everything was taken away from us, and we didn't know what we were now going to *do.*

To my surprise, God was about to rearrange how we did life and church. Those on staff began to realize how much we were *doing* as a church. Our identity, perhaps even our mission, was about *doing* church. It didn't take long for us to realize that perhaps we had been *straining at the oars* while *doing church*. We were exhausted and didn't know it. We went from program to program, Bible study to Bible study, worship service to worship service, from one event to the next. We were "making headway painfully."[7] As church leaders, we questioned whether we were making disciples or causing others to work out their faith by what they were *doing*, which caused them to be *straining at the oars*. The wind had been blowing against the church for a long time, but we continued to pick up the oars and painfully kept trying to move forward. *No wonder church leaders burn out, and church members stop attending.* It was time we needed to stop *doing* church and instead discover what it meant to *be* the church. It was time to put down the oars keeping us from *being* the church Jesus Christ gave his life for. We could no longer *do church,* or at least not in the way we had been *doing.*

Perhaps God would use this pandemic to stop us from *doing church?* Yet, who were we if we could not at least come together on Sunday mornings for worship? What were we going to *do?* As Christians, our identity as individuals in the church is largely based on what we do, rather than being a relationship with God, Father, Son, and Holy Spirit and with each other. We then wonder why our Christian faith doesn't mature or why the fruit of the Holy Spirit isn't being produced. We also wonder why the church or the Christian faith turns people off or why there is no growth by making new disciples. We seemed to have lost sight of what we are truly called to do; to love God and others while making disciples of all nations. The great commandment and the great commission.

---

[7]    Mark 6.48a, ESV

My suggestion is that the church in America has strayed from God's original mission, and that it has been *straining at the oars* for a long time. I heard that from pastors everywhere. No wonder pastors and church leaders burn out and church members stop attending. When did the church lose sight of what it means to *be* the church while *doing* church? We wonder why our lives seem void of true peace, happiness, and joy. Again, my thoughts are that it's because we have bought into this works-oriented way of faith that translates into our personal lives. We are becoming exhausted and weary from constantly *straining at the oars* of religion.

This pandemic has taught me, and many others, that we didn't even know we were *straining at the oars*. Trying to be *good people*, even *good Christians*, we've allowed the winds to beat against us, causing us pain and suffering. We were convinced that the more we worked, the harder we tried, and everything would work out for good. It's time we stop *straining at the oars* and recognize the storms, the winds, and the waves, that are beating against us. We need to take the necessary time to be still, allow Jesus into the boat, set down our oars, and let the Holy Spirit breathe life into our sails and our dry bones. It's not easy. Some habits are hard to break.

I pray this book will help you recognize the storms beating against you and the deceptions you may have bought into. The one big lie is that the only way to get through the *storms of destruction* and overcome adversity is by working harder and doing better. My prayer is that you might come to the realization that you have been *straining at the oars* for a long time without even knowing it and that you are able to admit that you can no longer live the same way, doing the same thing. Are you familiar with the definition of insanity, which is doing the same thing over and over and expecting different results? Something has to change. In being able to admit that your way has not been working and trusting in God to do a new thing, I believe the Holy Spirit will begin to bring revival, refreshment, and restoration to your soul.

Perhaps you have been rowing for a long time, and life seems to have been going well. Then, something happens in your life, and you suddenly realize that you've not moved very far, if at all. The years have gone by, the dreams have faded, the way of *doing* life has become difficult, and you're unsure why. The joy is not there, the passion is gone, and it's not about getting older. It's about realizing that you are tired of doing the same old thing and not experiencing any fruits from your labor.

It could be as simple as setting down the oars, letting Jesus into the boat, spending time with your Lord, and allowing the Holy Spirit to breathe new life into your *dry bones*. It may be you need to put things on pause for a day, a week, a month, or even a year. In time you will be ready to pick up the oars and join what God is doing, but with a greater sense of purpose and joy. By staying connected to the vine, Jesus, you will be able to bear fruit that lasts, sustains you, and even blesses those around you. You may find the condition of your heart, soul, mind, and body are such that you need professional help, or at least the help of some people you trust and respect, to help you navigate what you are going through. God will start putting wind into your sails and take you in a new direction as you set the oars down. Whatever it may be for you, it's time to stop *straining at the oars* and begin allowing the Holy Spirit to restore the joy of God's eternal love and salvation.

Many experiences in life create a sense of hopelessness, of struggle, where we are *straining at the oars* and don't even know it. I hope you will allow God to reveal the truths that can and will set you free. You might be struggling with depression. You might be living with guilt. Fear may be what's keeping you from enjoying the life Jesus Christ came to give you. Don't just read the chapters in this book to gain information—take your time. Linger for a while after reading something in the middle of a chapter and allow God to begin showing you what he wants to do with you to set you free.

As you read this book, I want you to imagine yourself sitting in that boat with the disciples. Take time even now to put yourself in the situation. Take a look at the water and notice the wind. What is going on? Who's in the boat with you? What does the boat represent? What is going on within your soul? Pay attention to your body. What are you *doing*? Perhaps there's a swell on the water, or a little ripple, indicating the wind is blowing. Maybe it's completely calm, or your boat is rocking uncontrollably, and you realize you're in the middle of a storm.

Sit there for a few moments, perhaps minutes, and just watch the situation. Watch for Jesus to appear on the water, or perhaps even in the boat. Notice how you respond to Him. Notice what Jesus does. Sit with that for a few more minutes.

Now, take time to pay attention to your personal current situation. What does the storm look like? What emotions are you experiencing? Is there anyone in the boat with you? Where is Jesus at the moment? Where would you like him to be? Don't read any further until you have spent enough time simply *being* in your situation without having to *do* another thing.

If you did that exercise right now, take time to write down what you saw and experienced. Record your emotions. Give it some details. Could you recognize what the storms are in your life? Describe what the storms and waves and wind looked like. Did Jesus appear? If so, how and when? What did He do? What did you do? Did anything change when Jesus appeared?

# Part One
## Straining at the Oars

The idea for this book came from the Gospel of Mark 6, where the disciples of Jesus were *straining at the oars*. It also comes from my own experiences of *straining at the oars*. The disciples were "straining at the oars because the wind was against them" or "making headway painfully, for the wind was against them."[8]

I wonder if to them, as it would have been to me, it felt like a *storm of destruction*. The picture I have in my mind of the disciples is them giving it all they had as they were rowing to the other side, but they were not getting anywhere very fast. They were *straining*. Plus, *it was the fourth watch*, about 5:00 am. Who knows how long they had been rowing, *straining at the oars*? I'm guessing they were exhausted. Perhaps as you pick up this book, you too are exhausted. You just don't know why.

It could be you are *straining at the oars* at this moment, or you know what it's like to *strain at the oars*. You've been there, done that. It could be that this book may not necessarily be for you at this moment. However, there may be someone you know or may come to know who could benefit from what you have gone through yourself and what these pages may pro-

---

8    Mark 6:48a, ESV

vide. What you discover while reading this book may provide insight for you to help someone else who is *straining at the oars*.

Whether this book is for you or someone else, I hope there will be a realization that it is time to stop straining and to set the oars down. It is time to let Jesus into the boat and allow him to take the yoke from you. Jesus knows that life, faith, and even ministry, can be exhausting. No wonder he once said, "Come to me, all you who labor and are heavy burdened, and I will give you rest. Take my yoke upon you, and learn from me, for I am gentle and humble in heart, and you will find rest for your souls." It's time to let Jesus *take the yoke from you*. It's been weighing you down for far too long. You have been *straining at the oars, making headway painfully*. You wonder why things are not getting better, why there is no joy in the journey, or why you are exhausted. Sometimes events, circumstances, and relationships can come against you, making it difficult to make any forward movement, progress, or even the smallest movement. There are moments, seasons, years, and decades where everything seems to be against you. It can seem as though you are constantly *straining at the oars*. It doesn't always have to be that way. God, the one who made the oceans, can calm the raging *storms of destruction*.

"You answer us with awesome and righteous deeds, God our Savior, the hope of all the ends of the earth and of the farthest seas, who formed the mountains by your power, having armed yourself with strength, who *stilled the roaring of the seas, the roaring of their waves, and the turmoil of the nations*. The whole earth is filled with awe at your wonders; where morning dawns, where evening fades, you call forth songs of joy."[9]

*Straining at the oars* may have nothing to do with whether or not you are making any progress. It may not have anything to do with trying to

<hr>

[9]    Psalm 65.5-8 NIV

move forward beyond your circumstances and struggles or even about you getting through the storms. You could be *making headway*. However, it is painful and lacks joy, and you could be unknowingly heading for disaster. It may be that there is more going on below the surface. It may not be about your circumstances or your inability to make progress. It could be that your *straining at the oars* is God's way of getting your attention. God may want you to recognize what is going on around you and what is going on inside you. You are *straining at the oars*, but for whatever reason, you ignore what is going on inside of you, how painful, exhausting, wearisome, and burdensome life has become. Something doesn't seem right, but you are not taking the time to investigate what it is. You are merely a survivor rather than truly being more than a conqueror. That's not the life Jesus wants you to live.

Jesus Christ came to earth to give everyone abundant and eternal *life*. He said, "The thief only comes to steal and kill and destroy. I came that they—you—may have life and have it abundantly."[10]

*Straining at the oars* is a way for the *thief*, the devil, to *steal, kill,* and *destroy* the life Jesus came to give you. If you do not do something about it, *straining at the oars* will overwhelm you, beat you down, and rob you of the peace, joy, and abundant life you will experience through Jesus Christ. Whatever you are going through, whatever it is that is beating against you, and you find yourself *straining at the oars*, you don't have to live that way anymore. Whatever seems to be defeating you and causing you to be weary and tired, you do not need to go through it alone. There is a new and better life available through Jesus Christ, the one who makes the waves and the winds be still. I hope this book will help you see the hope that is yours as you encounter Christ in the storms of life. Jesus Christ, Immanuel, God himself, is with you even in the apparent *storms of destruction*.[11]

---

10    John 10.10 ESV
11    Psalm 57.1 NIV

From the writings of CH Spurgeon in his devotional *Morning and Evening* are the following words that remind us that some of the greatest moments of growth in Christ can come through adversity:

> "Faith never prospers so well as when all things are against her: Tempests are her trainers, and bolts of lightning are her illuminators. When a calm reigns on the sea, spread the sails as you will, the ship does not move to its harbor; for on a slumbering ocean the keel sleeps too. Let the winds rush and howl, and let the waters lift themselves, though the vessel may rock and her deck may be washed with waves and her mast may creak under the pressure of the full and swelling sail, it is then that she makes headway toward her desired haven."

Spurgeon goes on to say:

> "Tested faith brings experience. You could not have believed your own weakness if you had not been compelled to pass through the rivers; and you would never have known God's strength if you had not been supported in the flood."

As you continue your journey, whether the waves are crashing over you or there is calm on the water, allow yourself to encounter Jesus. As I know from experience, life can turn upside down in an instant, with the next email, the next knock at the door, or the next late evening phone call. If all is calm right now, give praise to God, for there may be storms coming that only God is aware of. If all is calm right now, you perhaps are already aware of the storms that could be on the horizon. If waves are starting to swell and winds are stirring, don't grab the oars and take matters into your hands. Instead, use the time you have been given to read this book to settle in, take some deep breaths, and see how Christ will provide you with what you need to begin living life one moment and one day at a time. As you begin to read, perhaps do so by just reading one page or one chapter at a time.

As you read, allow yourself to pay attention to what God says to you. Listen for his still, small voice and watch for the winds of the Holy Spirit to blow upon the waters to stir within you a longing to encounter Christ. Bring about calm in your life as you begin to put down the oars and wait upon the Lord.

In the first part of this book, I will share just a few ways people strain at the oars. I am sharing how my life has constantly been *straining at the oars,* whether it's life in general, relationships, ministry, or even my faith. I hope my experience, my *straining at the oars,* will help you as you face your storms. My prayer is that you may learn how to encounter Christ in whatever you are going through now or in the coming days, months, or years.

# Chapter 1

# A CHANGE IN THE WEATHER

**W**e don't know how long the disciples were on the lake, rowing to the *other side*. We know that while they were on the lake, there was a change in the weather. The wind picked up. The waves started to wash over the sides of the boat. It was enough of a storm that the disciples were afraid of it. Meanwhile, as they began *straining at the oars*, it says that Jesus was on the shore, watching them, and it is said that he saw them *making headway painfully*.

When the weather changes and life throws a curveball and disrupts, interrupts, or turns our world upside down, Jesus may seem to be standing on the shore watching and doing nothing. But there is power in the fact that he sees us. He is not so far away, up in Heaven, that he cannot reach out and rescue you. He not only watches you, but he is with you. Know that whatever you are going through, God sees you. God knows you. God is with you. But, just like Jesus did not leave the disciples on their own, God will not leave you. He has not given up on you. Don't give up on yourself. Don't give up on God. At the same time, don't quickly fix things, attempting to make all things better. Don't believe that you have to simply work harder and begin to do things better, as though it is all up to you to make things right again.

As Jesus was watching the disciples, he did not wait for them to figure things out or begin rowing harder. He left the shore and went to them. They simply had to notice him, set down the oars, and let him in the boat. It's time to recognize Jesus in your midst, set down the oars, and let him guide you to the *other* side.

Keep in mind that the disciples were out in the water in the early morning hours, and it wasn't a calm body of water when Jesus came to them—there was a storm. The winds were beating against them, and the waves were raging. Still *straining at the oars*, the disciples thought they saw a ghost. They were even more afraid. Can you imagine? Who wouldn't be frightened in the middle of a raging storm, only to see a ghost approaching them? Jesus makes himself known and says, "It is I." Jesus is not just identifying himself to the disciples. He is reminding them of who he is. He is *I am* Jesus Christ, Immanuel, God in human flesh. The great *I am* is in their midst.

Then, Jesus entered the boat, and the *wind ceased*. It says in John's Gospel, "Immediately the boat was at the land to which they were going."[12] *Immediately* they reached the other shore. In the midst of your storm, as you are *straining at the oars*, Jesus is with you, and he is still able to command the storms to cease and the winds to be still. You are not alone. You have the *Great I am* with you. The One who made the heavens and the earth is ready to be welcomed into your life and into the midst of your storms. As you continue to strain at the oars, God wants you to know *I am the great I am, and I am with you.*

---

[12]    John 6.21, ESV

In 2020 the weather changed as the COVID-19 pandemic invaded our lives and the world. If that wasn't enough, the following year, I went through the biggest change in the weather I had ever experienced—divorce. However, this wasn't the first time I had experienced a change in the weather. Let me share part of my journey.

In 1986 I began doing full-time ministry as an ordained youth pastor. It was a ministry that saw much growth and fruit for nine years. As I look back at that time, as great of an experience as it had been—having all three of our daughters born during that time—it was very dark. I look back, and I believe I experienced depression. After nine years, I felt I had done all I could do as a youth pastor. I was ready for a change of scenery and ministry. I didn't know it at the time, but I had been *straining at the oars* of ministry. I had become exhausted. I accepted an Associate Pastor position in Yakima, Washington. It was a chance to receive new life. It was somewhat familiar, having graduated from Whitworth College—now Whitworth University—in Spokane, Washington.

The first time I preached to the Yakima congregation, my roommate from college was in attendance—he had grown up in that church. *I found him between services and told him I was not the same person he knew in college.*

I spent four very rich and rewarding years in Yakima. During that time, God gave me spiritual mentors, even someone I considered to be my spiritual *father*. However, a change of address didn't make things any easier. I was still the same person, the same husband, the same father, and the same pastor. The scenery had changed, but I hadn't. I realize now that I was not *straining at the oars* due to my external circumstances. I was *straining at the oars* because of internal struggles I had not been aware of at the time.

After four years in Yakima, I accepted a head pastor position at a small church in Southern California. It was like going home. Back to where I grew up and to what was familiar. Back to the LA Dodgers and Rams. Back to the beaches. Once again, it was a change of scenery, but the same old me. It didn't take long until there was a change in the weather, and try as I might, *straining at the oars* was not going to get me through the storm that was coming. After one year back in Southern California, I entered a deep depression—I will share more about that in another chapter.

At this little church in Southern California, there had been a lot of growth and lots of fruit. People came to the Lord. God moved in mighty ways. I had all the reasons in the world to be thrilled for what I thought would be an everlasting flourishing ministry. My depression was eventually managed through counseling, medicine, and a transformation within me that only the Holy Spirit could bring about. God sustained me through some very painful times. After ten years, I again stepped down from that position. I thought perhaps I was also leaving church ministry. I had no idea what I would do next. Eventually, perhaps too quickly, maybe a bit foolishly, I accepted a position an hour away to be a head pastor again. I went back to the denomination that ordained me. I thought I was ready to be back to what I knew. A change of scenery with a familiar setting was what I thought I needed. That lasted two years. If it wasn't such a toxic environment I could have taken everything personally, and probably would have fallen back into depression. I could have easily begun *straining at the oars* and powered my way through things, but I knew that wasn't what God wanted me to do. After a stint working at a Chic-fil-A restaurant, God called me back to Yakima to be a Hospice Chaplain.

Shortly after arriving back in Yakima, while serving as a Hospice Chaplain, I was invited to be the head pastor of the church where I had served several years earlier. As much of a blessing as it was, it wasn't smooth sailing at the beginning. Then, in my second year at the church, the pandemic began to surface. I honestly don't know how I survived the pandemic, being in *lock-down*, having to make church and ministry adjustments on the fly, and not having a sense of any progress. Life seemed to be on hold.

No matter how your life might be right now, there will be a shift in the weather at some point. What *was* will no longer be the same. What is to come may not be anything you could imagine. Even though many people wanted to get *back to normal* after the pandemic, *normal* was redefined. (Someone said *normal* is just a setting on a dryer.) After the pandemic and the storms of life, a new normal developed. The landscape will be changed, just like we saw after 9/11. *Still, I wouldn't say I like taking off my shoes and belt while going through transportation security administration.* No matter the *new normal*, I don't believe it will be a mere cosmetic change, like creating new and heightened security at airports.

There may be some cosmetic changes, like increased food deliveries, more attention to sanitizing stores and restaurants, and perhaps even how we conducted school and church. I also came to see a change taking place in our culture, for good and bad. There was a change in people's attitudes due to the pandemic and all the other chaotic and violent events everyone experienced during the pandemic. There was a greater realization of how we were already divided as a country. This realization was also evident within churches and among Christians. Families were divided over many issues. Yet, I believe the ugliness that has risen from the pandemic and other global events God is using to expose the lies and deception that have kept us *straining at the oars* in ways we didn't know existed in our lives, churches, and families. God will bring beauty out of ashes. However, the ashes will linger, perhaps for several generations.

As we celebrated Ash Wednesday, I was reminded that there is no Easter Sunday without Good Friday. There is no Resurrection without the Crucifixion.

Whatever you are going through right now, it may be exactly where God wants you to be in order to prepare you for what's coming next—the New Life—The Resurrection. However, God may need to strip you of all that has defined you up to now, exposing what has been going on below the surface, to pour *new wine* into your heart and soul that will begin to spill over into your entire life and relationships. And, as that new wine gives you a new hope there *will* be a breakthrough. But, keep in mind that a breakthrough means a change or a transformation. You may never get *back to normal*. To truly allow God to take you to the *other shore* means that you may have to leave behind the shore you were on originally. You may want to go back to the old shore. You may want life to get back to normal. I'm not sure I want to get back to what I thought was *normal.*

There's a *new normal* for all of us who are willing to stop *straining at the oars.* There will be a change in life, faith, and church. It's going to be a time of new beginnings. Perhaps we all need to put down our oars and stop doing life as we were used to doing it and allow God to reveal the *new thing* he is creating.

God says: "See, I am doing a new thing! Now it springs up; do you not perceive it? I am making a way in the wilderness and streams in the wasteland."[13] *Streams in the wasteland* sound a lot better than what the disciples were facing on the lake. Streams sound better than storms. However, God says he is doing something new and is *making a way* in the *wilderness* and the *wasteland. Wilderness and wasteland* are not descriptions of happy or fruitful places.

Fortunately, God's best work often comes when making something out of nothing, beauty out of ashes, order out of chaos, light out of darkness, and life out of death—*streams in the wasteland.*

---

13    Isaiah 43.19, NIV

So, what does that mean for the disciples? What does that mean for us? From an eternal perspective, we are all living in the *wilderness* and the *wasteland*. We are between God's first creation and his final creation, where there will be a new heaven and a new earth. We are between the first and final coming of Christ. During our time on earth, as we make our way across the lake or through the wilderness, there will be times God may use our storms of life to make us *lay down in green pastures* and *beside still waters*. Can he use a storm on the lake? Can he use the wilderness or the wasteland? Can he use COVID-19? Beyond debating whether God *causes* or *allows*, I know that he will use all things to advance his kingdom, test our faith, draw us closer to himself, and do *a new thing*. If we let him. If we pay attention to what he's doing. If we listen to his voice. If we dare to set down our oars. I love the fact that Jesus *made his disciples get into the boat*. The ESV says that Jesus "made his disciples get into the boat and go before him to the other side."[14] Jesus *made* them get into the boat in order for them to go to *the other side*. Yes, it's they are to go to the *other side* of the lake. However, it could be Jesus knew about the storm, and he will get them to the *other side* of the storm they will encounter. Or, Jesus will get them to the *other side* of their current and recent struggles. Or could it be something even more transforming, like getting beyond their current way of doing life and ministry? Once they were out in the water, and the winds came against them, they were *straining at the oars*, but this was all part of getting to *the other side*. Whatever storms we are in, whatever it is that is keeping us stuck or lost or confused, God will get us to the *other side*.

Sometimes, there will be a change in the weather. Our world is in a whirlwind, tossing us about, and the landscape in changed, perhaps forever. Even when all is going well, the winds can begin to blow. There will

---

[14]    Mark 6.45, ESV

be a shift in the atmosphere. Life was good. All was well. Kind of like Job. And then, out of nowhere, unexpectedly the winds begin to blow, and the storms pick up, and something out of our control rocks our world.

After having had a miraculous experience with Jesus, the feeding of the 5,000, the disciples were probably running on adrenalin. Jesus has them get into a boat, and tells them to go to the other side of the lake. I am sure they jumped in the boat and began rowing with great anticipation. They probably couldn't wait to see what Jesus was going to do next. But they soon realize Jesus wasn't getting in the boat with them. There's a shift in the atmosphere. Did they just lose their momentum? What was Jesus doing? Where was he going? Why wasn't he with them in the boat? Regardless, without any answers, not knowing where they were going, the disciples begin to row the boat.

They may have occasionally looked back at Jesus on the shore. *I can see him standing there, waving to them, maybe with a smirk on his face. He knows what's coming, even if they don't.* Soon, the winds began to pick up. It was time to row harder. There may have been a bit of fear, but they were fishermen; they knew how to row a boat, even in a storm. They've been in storms before. They have survived storms in the past. However, this storm may not have been like anything they had encountered before. All they knew to do was work with all their might to get to the *other* side before their boat capsized. This is when the author of the Gospel describes the disciples as *straining at the oars* and *painfully* making little progress.

That's what happens when life is on cruise control and all is going well. Then there is a sudden wake up call, a check in the spirit. Something is not right. I'm not referring to a mid-life crisis. I'm referring to that time when exhaustion sets in and life is a struggle, and we are weary from the journey. and we begin to realize that we have been *doing* things in the wrong way. We are working hard, yet there's no progress. There is no change. We have no sense of direction. We don't know left from right, up from down. Everything seems to be in a fog. We realize that something needs to change. It's then that we need to look on the horizon, investigate what is happening, listen to the Holy Spirit, and acknowledge that the abundant life Jesus came to give us has either disappeared, or is being sapped out of us little by little. Yet, too often, many of us just continue to spin the plates or juggle the balls, doing everything we can to keep doing life in our strength, in our familiar ways, even if it is killing us.

As I struggled during the pandemic to keep myself being productive, doing that which needed to be done still, in spite of working from home, I watched a webinar that talked about the emotional impact of this global pandemic and different types of *fatigue*—one of the fatigues mentioned was *unproductivity*. That made sense to me. I was fatigued because of what I believed to be a time of *unproductivity*. I was exhausted from dwelling on the lies that I was not doing enough. That was part of what was happening to staff members. They too felt as though they were not being productive. They were even questioning what everyone else was doing at home and how productive they were. Church leaders were questioning whether we were being productive. What they meant was, *are they doing anything?* The leaders were missing out on an opportunity to care for the staff, to check in with how they were handling things.

It's easy to get caught up in the need to be productive, and feeling guilty about not being productive *enough*. The truth was that during the pandemic there was perhaps an even greater productivity going on as people began to take care of themselves. That's not something any of us are good at. As a result, striving to be productive, no matter what is going on around us, neglecting the need to take care of ourself, not taking time to shut down once in a while, we can become exhausted, and possibly burn out. I found myself needing to encourage the staff, and even convince myself, that some of the best work we can do in such uncertain times was to put some things on pause, engage in prayer, reading, connecting with God and others. It wasn't easy to convince anyone, including me. And although it may have felt as though we were not *doing anything*, that time spent in silence, in prayer, in connecting with God and others, was the most productive thing we could possibly do.

However, from the get-go, there was this overwhelming concern to stay productive. After all, we had believed that ministry was all about *doing*. The lie was that to be still, to take time to reflect and process life an ministry, to take care of oneself was not productive. However, the truth, according to Psalm 46, is that during those times when our world is being torn apart, even when all is well, we are to *be still*, listen to God, pay attention to what He's doing, watch where He is leading us, and trust that He is going to take us to the *other side*. The pandemic was not a time to work harder, be more productive in order to prove we are doing our job. It was a time, perhaps a gift from God, to discover how to *do* life and ministry completely differently. It was time to stop *doing* church, and instead, it was a time to discover how to *be* the church.

It was a time to stop relying upon *doing* Christianity, and instead, to embrace what it meant to *be* a Christian. It was a time to stop identifying who we were by what we did, but to be identified by who we were in Christ.

Unfortunately, everywhere I looked, especially on social media platforms, I found myself experiencing guilt over not *doing* enough. It seemed like other pastors, churches, and friends were *doing* more. Some churches were gathering for worship in defiance of the lockdown orders. One family left our church because we were not open—we were not *doing* worship together. Some churches had people park in the parking lot and stay in their cars for worship and were given juice and crackers for communion. I saw one pastor sitting outside the church offering *drive-thru prayers*. I kept wondering, *is that what I should* be *doing?* I was *doing* a lot, but it didn't seem to be enough or even important. Our church was *doing* what we had to do at the time, though it may have looked like we weren't *doing* much. Perhaps we weren't posting it all on social networking platforms. Our church was doing a lot to care for one another and stay in touch with those most isolated. We also hit the pause button and began asking the questions. We continued to *do* ministry. Although there was an attempt to keep churches from *doing* ministry, nothing was going to keep the church from *being* the church, not even mandated lockdowns. It was the difference between being either Mary or Martha. *Mary and Martha were sisters who welcomed Jesus into their home. You can read the entire story in Luke 10.38-42. For now, let me summarize it as it is recorded in the NIV.*

As Jesus and the disciples enter the home of Mary and Martha, it says that Mary "sat at the feet of Jesus listening to what he said."[15] On the other hand, Martha was described as being "distracted by all the preparations that had to be made."[16] What Martha was doing, in and of itself, was not bad. However, we caught a glimpse of what was going on below the surface. She was upset that Mary was not helping her with the preparations. things."[17]

Instead, Mary was spending time *being* with Jesus while Martha was busy *doing* what she thought needed to be done to make Jesus feel welcome. After complaining to Jesus about her sister's apparent laziness, Jesus responds by saying, "Martha, Martha, you are worried and upset about many Jesus addresses what was going on inside Martha that kept her from enjoying the presence of her Lord. Although what Martha was doing was good, Jesus said to Martha, "Mary has chosen what is better."[18] Sometimes

---

15   Luke 10.39, NIV
16   Luke 10.40, NIV
17   Luke 10.41, NIV
18   Luke 10.42, NIV

we sacrifice the best, or the better, by doing what is good or what we think is necessary.

Theologian, Sinclair Ferguson says:

*"We have become such an activist generation of Christians that we can scarcely grasp that our first and greatest need is to be in this sense passive, being fed the good food of the word of God that we may 'be being transformed."*

Mary was listening to Jesus Christ, the word of God in the flesh. To sit and listen to the word of God may seem to the Martha's in our world as being passive, but remember, "the Word of God is living and active, sharper than any two-edged sword, piercing to the division of soul and of spirit, of joints and of marrow, and discerning the thoughts and intentions of the heart."[19] Ferguson also believes, "In our evangelical sub-culture there is a heavy emphasis on what we must do, including what we must do with our Bibles. But there is almost no emphasis that accords with the stress in the New Testament on what our Bibles will do to us.

During the pandemic, it was time for us as Christians and a church to be more like Mary, spending time sitting at the feet of Jesus. It was time to let God speak to us. Instead, it seemed as though we were racing around doing what needed to be done to make everyone feel comfortable and welcomed. At the same time, we ensured everybody was doing what they should be doing to help. For some reason, as Martha pointed out to Jesus, sitting at the feet of our Lord doesn't seem or feel productive. What a fallacy. Sometimes it is way more productive to be still and attentive to what God is trying to tell us.

So, even as things began to shift, and we were trying to listen to the voice of God, we kept trying to become innovative. We got right into the

---

[19]    Hebrews 4.12, ESV

*doing* mode of ministry. I even started writing a weekly blog and offering prayer gatherings through YouTube and Facebook. Was it motivated by guilt, a new way of *doing ministry*, or both?

I also had to come up with sermons earlier than normal to record them before Sunday to be posted online. It was challenging and yet invigorating. It also became exhausting. I wondered if what I was *doing* was making a difference for people or even for the kingdom of God.

As I woke up one morning and contemplated what I had to *do*, I realized why I wanted to write this book. People are exhausted from having to *do* the Christian life. People are exhausted just from doing life; only they don't realize it until they are forced into a time of isolation and solitude.

The demands of life, the need to keep up with everyone else, and the struggle of not having a life as others post on social media can be taxing. The same is true, if not more so, in the Christian life. We have all heard that Christianity is not about *doing* but rather about *being*. Perhaps you have heard a familiar illustration by Bill Hybels. He said that religion is spelled *do*, as though it's all about what we must *do* as Christian to be saved, and that Christianity is spelled *done*. Salvation is about what Christ has already *done* for us on the cross. I don't think most Christians buy into that concept. There are too many *doing* like Martha and not enough *being* like Mary.

I hope that this book will help raise awareness of how exhausting Christianity can be if we don't take time to sit at the feet of Jesus. The demands of the Christian faith can swell on the ocean and, without much warning, come crashing down like a tsunami, flooding every area of our being and all that surrounds us.

Before reading any further, perhaps you may need to check the weather. Do you sense there is a change in the air? Are you going through a season that is causing life as you knew it to be put on hold? Don't try to go back in search of the *good old days*. Don't try to grab the oars and just begin row-ing frantically to get through the storm. Set down the oars. Pay attention to what is going on outside and the storm that may be going on inside. Change is hard. Transition is difficult. It's not so much the change or tran-sition as it is the unknown. You may be going into uncharted waters. Hang on. Keep your arms and legs inside the vehicle at all times. You are in for an amazing journey. Like one of my favorite rides at Disneyland proclaims: "This here is the wildest ride in the *wilderness.*"

# Chapter 2

# THE BEATING WINDS

How often have you been in a situation, a season of life, or a period of ministry, when the winds seem to be beating against you, and you seem to be are *straining at the oars*? It appears the odds are stacked against you.

You just don't seem to get a break. You start making progress, but the winds come beating again, and you're thrown off course, knocked backward several years. It's as if you're starting all over again. You have to scramble to get your bearings, get back on track, and align things back in your favor again. When the winds pick up, and you seem stuck, lost, confused, how often have you taken matters into your hands, picked up the oars, put your head down, and just kept forging ahead? Have you ever felt compelled to keep rowing, no matter the cost? After all, being a Christian comes with a price—it wasn't meant to be easy. Right? So we may have been told. To be a disciple of Christ means that we are to *deny ourselves, pick up our cross and follow* him. That's true. However, for many, Christianity can often boil down to doing good and avoiding bad. That can be very exhausting, if not legalistic. It doesn't have to be that way. To follow Christ, to live the Christian life, to walk by faith can be and should be rewarding, if we surrender to God and lean upon Him during the greatest of storms. It's about paying attention to what God is saying, and watching for where God is leading, rather than having a knee jerk reaction when the winds beat against us. It's all about hearing the still small voice of God even in the midst of a hurricane, rather than forging on ahead in our own strength, doing the same things over and over, expecting different results. (Yep, that's the definition of insanity.)

Consider Abraham, the one who was so in tune with God that he was considered to have a heart after God, and was actually called a friend of God. He was so in tune with God that when he was told to leave his hometown, his friends and family, and to go to a place God would eventually reveal to him, there was no hesitation. At the time I'm sure it didn't make sense, and was extremely difficult. But, what if Abraham refused to follow the Lord? Abraham also followed the instructions of God to sacrifice his son Isaac on Moriah.

Joseph, one of the twelve songs of Jacob, endured great suffering. He was abandoned by his jealous brothers who sold him into slavery. However, if you know the story, God used the evil intentions of Joseph's brothers, meant to cause great harm to Joseph, and brought about a greater good, not just for Joseph, but for Joseph's brothers and father, and the rest of the Israelites who were suffering in a famine. We have no idea what God is doing all the time, why He allows suffering we have to endure, or why He calls us to follow Him through times in the wilderness.

Sometimes we are called to do what seems to be the impossible. Yes, sometimes there is a cost, a price to pay, a sacrifice and even loss. Yet, as you have probably heard many times: *God does not call the equipped. God equips the called.* If God calls us to leave all behind and follow Him, He goes with us and before us, and He will sustain us in order to accomplish His good and perfect will.

Jesus had to endure suffering Himself. In fact, there is nothing we experience in this world quite like what Jesus went through on our behalf. Being fully human, Jesus was also fully God. As a human he was not immune to suffering and temptation. With great agony, as He approached the night of His arrest, having been abandoned and betrayed by those He loved, persecuted for having done nothing wrong, Jesus wrestled in the flesh, wanting to be spared the inevitable. Imagine what would have happened if Jesus got up off His knees after wrestling with His Father, confronted those who were coming to arrest Him, and took matters into His own hands, in order to spare His life. Fortunately, as we know, He did the opposite. He surrendered to the will of His Father, humbled Himself to death on a cross. As with the life of Joseph, what the enemy thought was a victory for evil, God used to the death of His own Son to bring about an eternal victory, which is actually our eternal victory.

Yes, in this world, as Jesus told His disciples, there will be trouble. But, we are able to endure difficult times, seasons of great loss and sacrifice, knowing that Jesus, by His own humble surrendering to the cross, has overcome everything this world tries to use against us in order to beat us down and destroy us. When we encounter hard times, when we are going through the wilderness, we work hard, striving to be a better Christian, a more faithful follower of Christ, and an obedient disciple, following all the rules, and obeying all the commands. Unfortunately, if we do all in our own strength, we will find ourselves exhausted and weary and no good to anybody. Still, whenever the winds begin to beat against us, we continue to believe it's time for us to *press on*. We are to work harder, strive to be better, pull ourselves up by the bootstraps, and fight the battle on our own. It's as if that's what being a Christian is all about. It's up to us to bring victory out of defeat. It's up to us to fix things, to make things better, to prove that we are strong Christians. It's the Christian thing to do. It's what others expect of us.

Or, could it be that when the winds beat against us, God is using that time to change us, transform us, from the inside out. He's not asking us to give one more sacrifice, but rather to have a heart that seeks after Him, that humbly surrenders to His will, trusting that the battle belongs to Him, and the victory is already ours. It's not as easy as it seems. We cannot seem to break the cycle of defining Christianity by what we do, rather than trusting in who we are and who we are becoming in Christ.

There was a time when we owned a cat that did not enjoy being inside. He was an outdoor cat and would be gone for days, even weeks, at a time. After one of his adventures, he never returned. We thought that he had died, or worse, was killed. A few days before moving, we received a letter in the mail. It was from a member of the church I was serving. They happened to live by us. We didn't even know them. It turns out that our cat had been periodically been living with them. It turns out they had been feeding him—no wonder he hung out at their house. As we were about to move, we received a letter from them. They wanted us to do the *Christian thing* by retrieving him and taking him with us.

That has always stuck with me—the *Christian thing*. What book of the Bible did that come from? We never did retrieve the cat. After all, they were feeding the cat regularly. No wonder he was over at their house all of the time. Twenty years later, upon returning to that same town and church we left, that neighbor came up to me in church, introduced herself, and gave a little chuckle about that incident all those years ago. I did not know how to respond. I just smiled and nodded—the *Christian thing*. Inwardly I wasn't feeling like a good Christian.

When it comes to *straining at the oars*, as Christians, we wrestle with how to respond to certain winds that begin to beat against us, even the winds of someone else's *good intentions*. We struggle with *doing the Christian thing*, or at least the *right thing*, according to the expectations of others, even Godly people.

There could be winds of criticism that stir up a sense of inadequacy within us and create what seems like a Godly desire to be better by *doing the Christian thing*. The winds of criticism that beat against us can cause us to *strain at the oars* because we don't want to disappoint anyone or let them down. Often, the most painful criticisms can come from other Christians who have rather unfair expectations and demands. The winds could also be our expectations causing us to strain at the oars as we strive to be what we believe we are supposed to be as a good Christian. Perhaps motivated by fear and not wanting to upset God or others.

Or perhaps worse, we strain at the oars as we try to gain the approval of God and others. In trying to do better and be better, we tend to grip the oars harder and operate from a place of exhaustion and weakness and find ourselves not getting anywhere very fast. Jesus wants to take that yoke from us. The yoke we carry is often filled with a works-oriented Christianity, or what might be called *religiosity*. The yoke of Jesus is grace-oriented. I think Jesus knew how hard following him was going to be. Yet, I think he also knew that we would grow weary trying to do it in our strength. Even if we may not be exhausted physically, we become spiritually, emotionally, and mentally exhausted and weary. We do this as we keep *straining at the oars* of our rather legalistic and self-induced Christian labor. It keeps us from getting to the *other side*. We become weary and heavy burdened, striving to be a good Christian, doing the *Christian thing*, doing good works, instead of trusting in the grace of God.

Jesus wants to give us *rest for our weary souls.* He wants to remove those burdens from us and replace it with His yoke, which is easy. He's already done the heavy lifting. His yoke is a yoke of grace, not of works. Jesus also says that His *burden is light.* Our burden is to do good works, to do what is not merely Christ, but Godly. However, it is not a burden of obligation or duty, but a burden of grace, where what is expected of us is love to God and to love others.

While we are in the midst of the storm, or while we are going through the wilderness, Jesus wants us to experience rest and peace as we allow Him to lead us to the *other side.* Jesus wants us to rest in the freedom of God's amazing and beautiful grace and goodness, rather than *straining at the oars* of religiosity or works-oriented faith. He wants us to walk and live by grace, not by works.

Being a follower of Christ certainly comes with a cost. However, the cost of follow Jesus is not intended to rob us joy in this world. Rather, our call to deny ourselves, pick up our cross daily and follow Christ, is a life that will release an abundance of joy that only the Holy Spirit can provide, even as the winds try to beat us down. A work-oriented faith can prevent us from knowing the joy that comes with God's salvation. The enemy, Satan, tries to rob us of that joy by making us focus on ourselves, and our lack of goodness. Instead, we are called to focus on the goodness of God and the grace of Christ. Christians are called to follow Christ, to share in his suffering, not because God does not want us to enjoy life. The truth is that even as we share in the suffering of Christ, we also share in the life and resurrection of Christ, on earth and for eternity. The Apostle Paul wrote: "I count everything as loss because of the surpassing worth of knowing Christ Jesus my Lord. For his sake I have suffered the loss of all things and count them as rubbish, in order that I may gain Christ and be bound in him, not having a righteousness of my own that comes from the law, but that which comes through faith in Christ, the righteousness from God that depends on faith, that I may know him and the power of his resurrection, and may share his sufferings, becoming like him in his death, that by any means possible I may attain the resurrection from the dead."[20]

Many people have a hard time trusting or believing in God because they cannot accept the truth that God is good, or that He wants us to have a good life. Some people have told me they can't become a Christian or won't become a Christian because of that old saying, *God is a killjoy*. They believe that being a Christian means giving up everything they like.

Sinclair Ferguson writes, "To the unregenerate (non-Christian), God's will is inevitably unpleasant, simply because it is *his* (God's) will and not *their* will. They do not know that he wills much better for us than we can ever will for ourselves." It's even difficult for Christians to imagine that the burden of following Christ is light. It sounds like an oxymoron. A burden is a burden, cut and dry. While we are in this broken and imperfect world, there will be burdens. The Apostle Paul assures of this truth, "for while we are in this tent (our earthly body), we groan and are burdened, for we do not wish to be unclothed but clothed instead with our heavenly dwelling, so that what is mortal may be swallowed up by life."[21]

While living in our earthly body in an imperfect and broken world, we will experience burdens. However, following Christ is not a burden we are called to carry alone. Jesus took our sins and our burdens upon himself on the cross—he did the heavy lifting. Yes, we may still have to carry the burden or the consequences of our sins, but we do not need to be weighed down by guilt and shame. At the same time, God has given to us other believers, brothers and sisters in Christ, who can help us carry our burdens.

---

[20]    Philippians 3.8-11, ESV
[21]    2 Corinthians 5.4, NIV

We can trust that they will not give up on us or abandon us, but will do what they can to help us cross the finish line.

They won't enable us or simply feel sorry for us. With compassion and mercy they will suffer when we suffer, and they will rejoice when we rejoice. They won't jump into the pit with us, but they will lend a hand in pulling us up, even if it means speaking the truth in love and encouraging us to get even greater help than they can offer.

In the meantime, being a follower of Christ is costly, and it can be a burden. However, it also brings great joy knowing that what we endure in this world does not compare to what we shall gain in eternity. As the Apostle Paul said, "I consider that our present sufferings are not worth comparing with the glory that will be revealed to us."[22] In the midst of any suffering, our burdens can become lighter as we consider the joy of eternity that will be ours. Again, the Apostle Paul writes, "We always carry around in our body the death of Jesus, so that the life of Jesus may also be revealed in our body."[23]

Christians have a hard time trusting in the goodness of God as well. If they fully surrender everything, he will have them do something they don't want to do or even like doing. God might even send them to Africa or some remote, third-world country. Plus, if it's simple and easy and gentle and light, why are there so many difficulties being a Christian? The Christian life isn't always an easy path to follow. People sometimes ask, "Why do bad things happen to good people?" "Why does the grass always seem greener on the other side?" If that's what being a Christian involves, it's not worth pursuing. Some may even have a martyr complex—*did I make that up?* There must be pain, suffering, and sacrifice to be a true Christian.

---

[22]    Romans 8.18, NIV
[23]    2 Corinthians 4.10, NIV

It's like a badge of honor. Plus, if they aren't *working out their salvation*—another way of *straining at the oars*—doesn't that make God's grace cheap? I don't think that is what CS Lewis meant when he said, "We devalue our calling to discipleship when we settle for cheap grace." We make the grace of God *cheap* when we take advantage of it by doing whatever we want. We don't cheapen the grace of God by accepting the *rest* that Jesus wants to provide as we partner with him by following him as a disciple.

The Apostle Paul, the greatest receiver and proclaimer of God's grace, worked hard at his faith, not his salvation. He worked hard to *win the race*, not in his strength but by the grace of God. Paul did not want us to abuse God's grace by taking license to do anything we wanted, knowing God would always forgive us. Paul discovered that the grace of God was more than sufficient. Grace is a gift that keeps on giving and is what we all need, but we are sometimes too proud to accept. Instead, we'd rather keep *straining at the oars*, as though it's up to us and us alone to work out our salvation.

Many times we are driven by a false guilt, a false belief that we are not worthy of God's grace. However, that's what grace is all about. None of us are worthy or deserving of God's grace, and certainly not deserving of forgiveness. Unfortunately, false guilt is one of the many winds that beat against me. Guilt can be a good motivator if it's appropriate guilt. My experience tells me that most people don't pay attention to the good or appropriate guilt. It's mostly false guilt, unnecessary guilt, unwarranted guilt that seems to beat against most people. That kind of guilt weighs us down by convincing us that we are not good enough or that we are not doing enough good things. Good guilt, convicting guilt from the Holy Spirit, can cause us to stop and pay attention to what is going on within us during times when we are *straining at the oars*, or *making headway painfully*.

Let me go back to the *wilderness* and *wasteland,* seasons in life when we feel stuck, as though we are not going anywhere, *making headway painfully.* It could be that is where God wants us, where we need to be, for a season, not forever. It is in *wilderness* and *wasteland* that God is at work doing a new thing, a better thing, more than we can imagine at the time. So, if you are in a place where you feel stuck, don't try to get out of the *wilderness* or *wasteland.* Don't attempt to get to *the other side* too quickly. There is a lot to learn as the winds keep beating against you.

Psalm 46 says that it's exactly when the winds are beating against you, or when the waters are tossing you about, that God says: "Be still, and know that I am God."[24] It's not a time to do nothing, or to be passively waiting, but to actively engage with God in prayer, listening for Him to speak into the depth of our soul, in order to receive what we need in a dry and weary time.

We'll discuss that later, but spend time being still right now. Quiet the other voices trying to distract you, and begin listening for God's still small voice. Don't *do* anything. Just *be still.* It's not easy. Then, in your stillness, pay attention to the blowing winds. Acknowledge where they are coming from. Are the winds internal or external? Is it fear, anxiety, conflict, or finances? Are there beliefs you adopted, perhaps ones that were even taught to you by good meaning Sunday school teachers and pastors, about what it means to be a *good Christian?* Or what is *expected* of you as a Christian? Are the winds that keep coming against you the echo of words spoken to you long ago, even by your parents? Are the winds reminding you of your weaknesses and shortcomings? Are they stirring a pang of false guilt within you? Are they reminding you of past failures where you have already sought forgiveness?

---

[24]    Psalm 46.10, NIV

Pay attention to the emotions you are experiencing. Are you anxious, angry, sad, depressed, or oppressed? What are you telling yourself about this time in your life? Did someone ever tell you that you were not good enough, that you had to work harder, that you would never succeed? Are those lies blowing against you? Do you still believe them to be true? Have you convinced yourself that what others have said about you is true?

As you recognize the winds blowing and how they are affecting you internally and externally, listen to the voice of God saying, *be still and know that I am God.* Let God speak truth into those winds.

Begin to exchange those lies for the truth of Christ that sets you free and reclaim the promises of God. When you begin to believe that you are not enough, claim the truth that Jesus is enough. As you become convinced that to be the person that God wants you to be, you must work harder and be better, claim the truth that God's grace is sufficient, even in times of weakness. When you question God's goodness as the winds blow, believing he has left you on your own, remember his promise never to leave, forsake or abandon you. Remember that God is not only with you, but he also is on your side, and if God is for you, nothing, not even the fiercest of winds, can separate you from the goodness of God. Claim the truth that God is in control, all-powerful and all-knowing. Trust that he uses all things to bring about his good and perfect will for you. During any raging storm, the truth about God—the Father, Son, and Holy Spirit—will set you free from the chains. They will help you set down the oars and experience the peace that passes all understanding. Watch the winds of doubt, fear and false guilt begin to settle down. As God told Moses, he tells us, "My presence will go with you, and I will give you rest."[25]

---

[25]     Exodus 33.14, NIV

When Jesus said, "Come to me all who are weary and burdened and I will give you rest,"[26] he referred to his disciples under the yoke of the legalistic and self-righteous Pharisees. It could refer to those who have allowed themselves to be oppressed by the legalism and false guilt that comes from it, as well as physical and emotional strain.

At another time, when Jesus was teaching in the synagogues, traveling from town to town, he saw the people as *harassed and helpless, like sheep without a shepherd.*[27] Jesus knows our souls better than we do. He knows that we are *harassed and helpless*, weary, and exhausted. He sees into people's souls plagued by false guilt, striving to please God and others by meeting self-imposed expectations. Or, rather than trusting in the grace of God, the temptation is to meet the spoken and unspoken expectations of others and perform for God in order to keep him pleased with you. The winds of false guilt and legalism are beating against us, preventing us from experiencing and tasting the goodness of God. We are exhausted, tired, burdened, and weary. It's time to begin putting down the oars in order to receive the rest that only God can give us.

You may not even be aware of the winds beating against you for years, if not your entire life. You're exhausted, and you don't know why. You're doing the best you can, but it doesn't make any difference. Some of the winds beating against you may come from within yourself. Some of the winds may come from outside of you. The winds beating against you could be due to an unhealthy and toxic relationship, or circumstances that are not in your control. Whatever those winds are in your personal life, they may be keeping you from advancing closer to God's preferred future and arriving at the *other side* of what you are currently going through.

---

[26]    Matthew 11.28, NIV
[27]    Matthew 9.36b, NIV

In the next few chapters I will share of what I have encountered that has prevented me from becoming who God is calling me to become, and keeping me from arriving at the *other side*. I don't share any of it to make you admire me or pity me. I just want you to know that I am writing from personal experiences. I will share some of ways I have been *straining at the oars* as the winds were beating against me. Hopefully what I share will help give you understanding and clarity to what you are going through. If anything, it may help you come to realize and acknowledge that you are not alone. Although we are all unique, and our circumstances are not identical, we can all gain a better perspective from hearing what others have endured, and hopefully how they were able to weather the storms and get to the *other side*.

# Chapter 3

# THE PERFECT STORM

I n 2017 my life took another turn. When I look back at what happened, I tell people it was the *perfect storm*. According to *Oxford Languages*, a perfect storm can be defined in a couple of ways. One is a particularly violent arising from a rare combination of adverse meteorological factors. Another definition of a perfect storm—more suitable to what I'm referring to—is a particularly bad or critical state of affairs arising from several negative and unpredictable factors. *Miriam-Webster* defines a perfect storm as a critical or disastrous situation created by a powerful concurrence of factors. My life was about to have a combination of *negative and unpredictable* events that would lead to radical changes over the next several years. I didn't know it at the time, but rather than being a violent or severe storm, it was something others have called God's *severe mercy*. If it weren't for these rather unusual or God-ordained events, who knows what my life would be like today. Something had to change. God would use several events to set me free from what was holding me back from experiencing the fulness of His grace, love, joy, and hope. However, it didn't come without pain. I had no idea where it would take me, but the winds were starting to pick up, and the waters were beginning to roar.

Sometimes, God has to allow things to get so complicated and even difficult for me to let go of my plans. There are times when God has to rip what I am clinging to out of my hands. I'd rather not get to the point where he has to rip them from my hands. Fortunately, before God had to pry my hands open, I had concluded that I had to let go of ministry. After years of *straining at the oars* of a church, I resigned from my position as pastor. Other situations in my life led to my resignation, but it was all part of the *perfect storm*.

As I headed into a new season of life, I had no ministry and no church ministry responsibilities. It kind of felt good. I had no idea that I had been *straining at the oars* for several years as a pastor, and it had taken its toll on me. Looking back at everything that took place, I realize that I could have been shipwrecked. If I kept going in the same direction, doing the same things, I could have crashed and burned. Yet, God rescued me when I resigned, redirected my bearings, and the Holy Spirit began to breathe life into my sails.

I began to realize that how I had been *doing* life and ministry would not be the same from now on. God was going to use this time to begin a transformation. I don't know why, but I was calm and at peace, with a sense of confidence that God would use the perfect storm for my good according to his perfect will. Perhaps, secretly, deep inside, I was a bit fearful. But I was more curious than anything. A door had been closed, and other doors were opening. Where was God leading me? What was I going to *do* next? Even when I had some ideas or was beginning to figure them out, God would lead me through other doors that were opening, doors I had not even considered before. There were doors about to open that I didn't even know existed.

Looking back at it all, it's as if God put me in the boat and said, *go to the other side*. Little did I know what would be on the other side of all this. I didn't know what would happen while in the boat amid the *perfect storm*. There I was, in the boat, out on the water, wondering what I was going to do next. I didn't even seem to have any oars. I was totally at the mercy of God for what was going to happen next. I had to trust God with my future. There didn't seem to be anything I could do at the moment. No wonder Jesus tells us not to worry about tomorrow. It was enough to know that God was with me today, just as he had been with me yesterday and would be with me tomorrow. Without any oars, I was unable to control my destiny. Eventually, there was what I hoped was the prompting of the Holy Spirit. It was as if the Holy Spirit was putting the breath of God into my sails, spirit, and life. Slowly, I began to glimpse the future, or so I thought. First, my life and ministry coach invited me to join him on a trip to Spain. He had been coaching me for several years. He became a good friend and still is to this day. He not only coached me while I was a pastor, but he has also trained me to be a coach. At one point, I thought God would use me as a coach for pastors and churches, and he has in various ways, although it hasn't been to the extent I imagined.

The purpose of the trip to Spain was to train missionaries to coach their leaders. I helped demonstrate coaching practices and techniques. Part of the training involved the missionaries practicing what they were being taught. One of the missionaries was given a chance to role-play *coaching* me. It was more than role-playing. Being still raw from leaving the church, I used that opportunity to process my next steps. What came out of that session was a clear word from God saying that I was not done with ministry. God was still going to use me. I had no idea what that meant, except I thought coaching was what God was perhaps calling me to do in my next season of ministry.

At the same time, I didn't know that another gentleman would be in Spain with us. He trained the missionaries on how to develop a new way of making disciples in their context by finding a *person of peace*. That type of discipleship began to give me a hope of a future ministry I could get my teeth into as well. I started to feel the wind in my sails. Unfortunately, I started to pick up the oars, and I again began rowing independently. *Thank you, God, I got it from here.*

When I returned to the United States, I was ready to *do* church by making disciples who make disciples. What a novel idea—*that's meant to be sarcastic.* How quickly I forgot about coaching. I eventually got some friends together from the church where I had just resigned. *Call me crazy—it's hard to let go of the past. It's hard to allow God to be at the helm.*

It wasn't long before a few of my friends met at my house. I shared with them what I had learned in Spain. In all honesty, what I was doing was grabbing hold of a set of oars and foolishly believing that I was beginning to make progress. Well, that did not last long. *What was that all about?* I still don't know. Was that just a waste of time and energy? Did I misread God? Did I go to Spain just to be told that God was still going to use me? What did that mean? Was it going to be *doing* church by making disciples who make disciples? I was going to do it differently. I was not going to be the same pastor I was before. *So, what was that all about?* I have always said that God doesn't waste anything. Well, as I look back, I know nothing was wasted. I just had more learning to do.

After realizing that this new way of *doing church* was not what God was preparing me for, another breeze began to blow. Was God now going to reveal to me his plans at this time?

While visiting with a friend from my former church, I began sharing my experience in Spain. I talked about how I hoped to *do* church in this new, yet old, way by making disciples. As I was sharing the concept, she began to get a smile on her face. She knew what I was talking about. Having been to Ethiopia on several occasions with a ministry based in San Diego, my friend said, "That's exactly what we do in Ethiopia." She wanted me to meet a gentleman heading up these trips to Ethiopia.

My initial response was a big solid *no*. I had been on several mission trips. I had been to Africa four times, twice each to Kenya and Rwanda. I was not convinced that God was calling me to go to Ethiopia. Yet, before I knew what was happening, I was meeting with the president of the mission organization and discussing not only going to Ethiopia but joining their ministry.

I ended up going to Ethiopia and learned how they do ministry while also being trained to take a team myself eventually. So, I picked up the oars and started rowing once again. It seemed as though this was where God was leading me. If I'm honest, which is hard for me to do sometimes, I wasn't waiting on God, listening to him, or watching for his movement. I just stopped sitting around *doing* nothing.

Unfortunately, even though it was an amazing experience in Ethiopia, it was not something I felt God was calling me to do going forward. So, there was more sitting, waiting, watching, and wondering what God was up to. Was God just keeping me busy as he continued to put things in place? I felt that I was having a tough time discerning what God was doing. Perhaps I hadn't completely let go of the oars. I was still in control, pretending to believe God was in charge.

My *perfect storm* wasn't over. I trusted God knew what he was doing, even though I still had no idea what I would do. Money was running out, and I needed some kind of employment, even if temporarily.

Shortly after, I had a job interview. It was another open door, and I felt God would use it for my future. I had applied for a position at a local Chick-fil-A restaurant. I was intrigued by this Christian organization that was closed on Sundays. I got an interview, and it went well. They hired me straight away. The owner and manager felt I had the potential for upper management. They saw me as a mentor for the other staff members—most of them were in their 20s. Again, I started to have hope that God was up to something. I started to sense the wind blowing in my sails. I would use my coaching skills to mentor people while being groomed for management at Chick-fil-A.

The work was intense, and at times I was way out of my league trying to keep up with multi-tasking 20-something year-olds. I learned a lot. I learned how to clean children's play equipment. I learned how to take food to customers. I learned how to compact cardboard and heft it into the trash unit. I learned how to make their famous lemonade—although one time, I made several batches without sugar. I learned how to make shakes and ice *dream* cones—yes, ice *dream cones* are a Chick-fil-A thing. I learned how to clean bathrooms until the porcelain was sparkling. I learned that the drive thru area of the restaurant is a jungle, and I could not keep pace with all the orders. Fortunately, the owner also realized that the drive-thru was not a good place for me to work.

Working at Chick-fil-A was a gratifying experience for me. I have never worked with or for such devoted, passionate, fun-loving people who were basically servants. I had never seen anything like it in church. I was genuinely humbled as friends would come in and see me cleaning tables and taking out the trash. I was the oldest person on staff, and the team members loved me—I had never been loved so much by co-workers before. They even took care of me as I threw up after a roller coaster ride during a team-building day at a local amusement park.

Little did I know that Chick-fil-A was just another piece of the puzzle that God was using to train me, equip me, and transform me, even as he was breaking me. I became a better person, and even a better pastor, for having served at Chick-fil-A. I didn't get promoted to management and had to figure out what to do next, as the salary would not suffice. What I didn't know at the time was that God was using my employment at Chick-fil-A to continue to mold me and prepare me for the future.

In the meantime, I sent my library of church and ministry books to the Philippines, where a friend was developing a ministry to train pastors. I didn't need them anymore. I honestly did not believe I would be back in church ministry. Yet I kept looking into various church positions suitable for my gifts, skills, and experience. I even applied to some churches and was gently turned down. I thought perhaps I'd make a good executive pastor.

Then, while praying and seeking God's call, I felt led to consider going back to Yakima, Washington. I had served as an associate at a church in Yakima 20 years earlier. After only four years in Yakima I had left to take a position as head pastor in Southern California. Although I wasn't in Yakima very long, it was experience. Going back to Yakima seemed to make sense. But, what about a job? I couldn't move without having something in place. The church I served at as an associate had a head pastor. Maybe they would be interested in me serving as an executive pastor. Oh, the plans I began to make in my head. Nothing wrong with dreaming, right? *Be careful what you wish or pray for.* It makes me think of two disciples, James and John, brothers. They are referred to as "sons of thunder."[28] Jesus had just told the disciples that he was going to die.[29] James and John responded rather selfishly. *More about that later in the book.* Knowing that Jesus would be going to heaven, they said, "We want you to do for us whatever we ask."[30] And, what did they ask? They said, "Let one of us sit at your right and the

---

[28]  Mark 3.17, NIV
[29]  Mark 10.32-34, NIV
[30]  Mark 10.35, NIV

other at your left in your glory."[31] They had no idea what they were asking. Jesus said to them, "You don't know what you are asking." Jesus said to them, "Are you able to drink the cup I drink…?" Again, foolishly and arrogantly said, "We can." *Really?* Jesus, perhaps knowing that they were not yet truly able to drink the cup he was about to drink, said to them, "You will drink."[32] When we begin to imagine what we want to do or want God to do for us, we need to be ready to *drink the cup*. It might be wiser to wait for God to roll out his plans and share what he wants us to do with us. His ways and his plans are always much better than ours.

Even more than that, if we must *drink the cup* to do what God wants us to do, we need to believe and trust that God is the one who empowers us and equips us to *drink the cup*. God alone gives us what we need to do and what he calls us to do, even if we experience adversity and hardship. The psalmist knew this to be true when he wrote, "You who have made me see many troubles and calamities will revive me again; from the depths of the earth, you will bring me up again."[33]

Notice the great wisdom found in the Heidelberg Confession:

Question 26: What believest thou when thou sayest, "I believe in God the Father, Almighty, Maker of heaven and earth?"

Answer: That the eternal Father of our Lord Jesus Christ *who of nothing made heaven and earth, with all that is in them; who likewise upholds and governs the same by his*

---

[31]    Mark 10.37, NIV
[32]    Mark 10.39, NIV
[33]    Psalm 71.20, ESV

*eternal counsel and providence* is for the sake of Christ his Son, my God and my Father; on whom I rely so entirely, that I have no doubt, but he will provide me with all things necessary for soul and body and further, that he will make whatever evils he sends upon me, in this valley of tears turn out to my advantage; for he is able to do it, being Almighty God, and willing, being a faithful Father.

As I considered everything that led me to where I am today, I found myself asking, "What if?" What if I didn't ask God to do what I wanted him to do? Was I prepared to *drink the* cup that awaited me? I have come to no longer ask the *what if* question. Rather, I am asking God, "What is it you have for me at this time? What is it that you are preparing me for next? What do you want me to learn from everything that has happened? How are you growing me and changing me? How are you going to use everything to bring about your good and perfect purpose?" In the eternal plans of God, he who makes all things work together for the good of those who love him, the *what if* questions don't change things. Yet, God never changes. God is sovereign, and he is always faithfully in control. He knows his plans for us, to prosper us and not to harm us—it may not always seem that way, but it's true.

As a result, I continually claim the promise, "And *God is able* to make all grace abound to you, so that having all sufficiency in all things at all times, you may abound in every good work."[34]

I have realized that when I try to make my plans without seeking God's plans, I cannot make progress, move forward, and experience joy and peace. Yet, even during my ill-fated plans, I have also believed that God can use all things to bring about his good and perfect will for my life. I have come

---

[34]    2 Corinthians 9.8, ESV

to trust that even when I make my plans, as Scripture says, I have to allow God to guide my steps.[35] It's always better to allow God to make my plans first. It always goes much better when I ask God to show me the way. "For you are my rock and my fortress; and for your name's sake you lead me and guide me."[36] "You make known to me the path of life; in your presence there is fullness of joy; at your right hand are pleasures forevermore."[37]

Ok, back to my plans for God. *Oh, I love to tell God what I want to do—even more so, I love to tell God what he should do.* As I began to think about my plans, Yakima seemed like a good place to move back to. A college friend I served with in Yakima 20 years earlier had moved away, but he was now back in Yakima. He was the Spiritual Director at the local hospital. I decided to reach out to him. I asked him what he was doing and how he liked his new calling after being in the church ministry most of his career.

It was a good conversation, and he recommended looking into a place in town that may need a chaplain. Although that place was a dead end, it got me thinking. I started looking into other chaplain positions in Yakima. One came up at the hospital where my friend was working. I wondered if that was the position he took. They just hadn't deleted the position from the employment board. I didn't get my hopes up. However, I investigated and found out that it was not my friend's position. They were looking for a hospice chaplain. I applied, was interviewed, and was hired almost immediately. This job seemed to be exactly what God was preparing me for.

It had been one year since I resigned from the church. It had been a year of ups and downs and silence. A year of hopes and dreams and expectations that never came about. It was a year of sorrow and confusion. Yet, there was a peace that only God could give me in its midst. In a matter of weeks,

---

[35] Proverbs 16.9, NIV
[36] Psalm 31.3, ESV
[37] Psalm 16.11, ESV

I moved to Yakima. My wife stayed behind to finish the school year as a substitute teacher and sell the house—eventually, she joined me.

My journey was not over. While living in the basement of some friends, I felt very alone and out of place. I wondered if I had made a mistake. Like with Chick-fil-A, being a hospice chaplain had its challenges and blessings. Those who served in hospice were passionate, loving, caring, humble people. It truly is a calling and not for everybody. As the months went by, little did I know God was using that time to prepare me for what was next.

The church I previously served at in Yakima 20 years ago was going through a transition. They reached out to me. At first, it seemed like I might use my coaching skills to come alongside the leaders and the head pastor. Then it appeared that maybe I would become the executive pastor. I was visiting the church off and on. There were many familiar faces, but something did not seem right. I visited other churches, only to be disappointed. I felt even more alone. I wasn't sure I would find a church that seemed to be a place where I could feel at home.

One day I received a phone call. It was from an elder at the church in Yakima I served 20 years earlier. The leaders had asked the head pastor to take some time off and asked if I could preach on a couple of Sundays. Without any real hesitation, I said *yes*. Then, after having preached two times, I got another call from the same elder. *Are you available to help at our Christmas Eve service?* I didn't know what that initially meant. The pastor was back from his time off. What is it would I do for Christmas Eve? Without anyone knowing anything at the time, the pastor would resign, and the elders wanted me to do the complete Christmas Eve service, message, and all—both services. That Christmas Eve was spectacular.

Long story short—*ok, it hasn't been short*—I was invited to be the church's *interim pastor*, which meant leaving my hospice chaplain position. It was not the easiest choice as I had been enjoying working with the hospice team. I hadn't been serving in a church for a couple of years and had enjoyed having Sundays open to do and go where I pleased. I did enjoy preaching, though—it gave me life, and I felt reinvigorated. It felt as though it was what I was meant to do, unlike ever before.

I said goodbye to being a hospice chaplain to become the interim pastor at a church I fell in love with again. It was the one church where God had grown me the most and the one church I did not leave due to painful situations.

After a year of being the interim pastor, I was given an invitation to be their permanent head pastor. Wow. I did not see that one coming. I secretly imagined being the head pastor but didn't want to get my hopes up. It had been two years pretty much to the date since I resigned from being a pastor in California. It had been quite an adventure. This was not a complete wilderness experience but a growing and maturing experience. I know that God used everything that happened over the years to shape, mold, and grow me into who I am today.

So, enough about me.

What about you? How does this apply to you?

I don't know your situation. I don't know where you find yourself as you read this book. Whether you are sailing along smoothly or have encountered some storms of your own, God is always at work. If all is well, you know that everything can be turned upside down instantly. A friend has said that we're all one phone call away from our lives being thrown into chaos, desperation, confusion, and pain. That's not exactly what they said, but you get the point.

Think about whether you are in a *perfect storm* or sense that you may be heading into one. Everything seems to be hitting you all at once. You're in a panic trying to figure out what God is up to or how you will navigate through it all. You are not the first one to be experiencing what you are going through, and you will not be the last. Perhaps God will use what you are going through to help someone else at some point. Do not give up hope on whatever this world is throwing at you or whatever has been taken out from under you. Do not despair. God is with you. God is in control. He has you. He is at work. Watch for what He is doing. God can use the mess your life seems to be in right now, in order to get rid of the old and to bring in something completely new. He says, "Behold, I am doing a new thing; now it springs forth, do you not perceive it? I will make a way in the wilderness and rivers in the desert."[38] God uses all things to bring together his plans for his kingdom and for His glory, as well as to give to you more of the abundant life Christ came to give all who believe. God does not waste anything.

It may feel like the *perfect storm* to you right now. Life has thrown you a curveball and things aren't making much sense. All the odds are stacked against you. There may even be great pain that you are experiencing in the midst of it all. You may seem as though you are heading for a shipwreck. It doesn't necessarily mean you have stepped away from God's will and experiencing the consequences of poor decisions. It also doesn't mean you need to frantically find answers and solve problems. Don't pick up the oars and start rowing. You may need to take some time to listen to God, confess anything that is brought to your attention, or simply ask God to reveal to you what He wants you to discover at this time.

Remember, in Mark 6, in the ESV, it says the disciples were *making headway painfully*[39]. They were doing what Jesus told them to do—rowing to the other side of the lake. It wasn't going to be a pleasure cruise, a three hour tour, or a pleasant day on the lake. It was going to be excruciatingly painful. They were not going to be getting anywhere very fast. Yet, it could

---

[38]  Isaiah 43.19, NIV
[39]  Mark 6:48, ESV

be that they were right where God wanted them to be—in the middle of a storm, a perfect storm, one that would cause them to trust in Jesus more than ever. Maybe that's exactly why you are experiencing what you are going through right now.

If you are in the middle of a storm, don't start to rationalize, justify, analyze, or even solve life's problems. Don't play the *what if* game. Set down the oars and pay attention to what is happening around you. You may be right where God wants you. However, be ready to make some adjustments. God may just be taking you through a transition. I will address that in the next chapter. In the meantime, God may be asking you to get out of the boat and to begin walking on water, trusting him, relying on him, and depending on him to deliver you to the *other side* of the storm.

# Chapter 4

# OARS OF TRANSITION

Little did I know that I would be going through another major life transition when I began writing this chapter. I was going through an unexpected divorce at the time. Talk about uncharted waters. I was going to call this chapter *The Tides of Transition*. However, going through a major transition like divorce feels more like a tsunami. I have this picture in my head where I see an actual tsunami on the news, with people hanging on to a tree they climbed to avoid the rushing waters. That is what it felt like for me. I was hanging on tightly to everything I knew, but I had to start letting go, and I was afraid of where the rushing waters and the raging winds were going to take me. Where would I eventually land?

On one occasion, when I was visiting a city on the coast, I noticed signs about tsunami warnings. I actually heard a tsunami alarm go off, but I had no idea what it was until later. I guess they test the system once in a while. I noticed there were also evacuation signs telling what route to take in case there is a tsunami. The routes are always going to take you to higher ground. A tsunami is usually created by some kind of quake out in the ocean. As the result of some quakes, seismologists can alert officials of a potential tsunami.

Just like those quakes in the ocean, there are also warning signs in life that make us aware that something is going on. Maybe it's the financial uncertainty at your place of employment, people being laid off, telling you that you could be next. There could be indications that something is not right physically, or that a relationship is all of a sudden on edge. There are signs that could create a sense that perhaps danger is coming. We are not always prepared for the tsunami of transition that comes our way. Transitions came come out of nowhere, unexpectedly, or as a slow swell on the horizon that you watch coming to the shores of your life. Unfortunately, unlike the evacuation routes in coastal cities, there are no signs telling us where to go and what to do.

Transitions in life can seem like a tsunami. They can send us into panic mode. But, it doesn't have to be that way. Transitions can be what God uses to help us stop clinging to that which is keeping us from making any kind of headway. Terry B. Walling, in his book *Stuck: Navigating Life and Leadership Transitions*, defines a transition as "… an in-between period in the life development of a Christ-follower." The truth is that transitions affect all people, no matter their age, faith, or life situation. He says, "Transitions bring closure to the past in order to move forward to the next stage of personal development. Transitions are characterized by a prolonged period of restlessness, self-doubt, lack of motivation, stagnation, diminished confidence, lack of direction, distance from God, isolation, relational conflict and tension, lack of effectiveness, and a struggle to stay focused and motivated." I don't know if this is an exhaustive list. You might experience other signs of being *stuck* or in a transition. One thing to notice is that Walling says it is a *prolonged period*.

Everyone has moments of self-doubt or times of isolation. That doesn't necessarily mean you are in a transition. If you experience indicators or warning signs for a continued period, perhaps years, then you may be in a transition. It is often hard to know when a transition begins.

Walling describes the different transition phases as entry, evaluation, alignment, and direction. If you have gone through any transition in life, you may be able to pinpoint each phase. Not everyone can recognize when they are in the *entry phase* of a transition. It may become apparent that someone is in a transition as they begin to evaluate what is going on in their current situation. The *direction phase* is where one begins to surrender to what the new future will look like while letting go of the past. This may include failures and successes, pain and suffering, habits and patterns that no longer work, or perhaps even a career path. Transitions come in all shapes and sizes.

Many transitions in life are normal, like graduating from high school, getting married, being promoted in a job, or even retirement. Transitions that cause us to *strain at the oars* are the ones that come unexpectedly and seemingly unwarranted. It could be the loss of a job, a divorce, a death of a loved one, or even a diagnosis of an incurable illness. Some transitions are a result of choices we make, while others are because of choices made by others. Some transitions we control, while others are out of our control. When I recently reviewed my life, marking some of the transitions that I have gone through, I realized that by the age of 17, my family had moved seven times. I had attended three different high schools. I have realized that my upbringing created within me a resilient spirit. It also prepared me for many more transitions in my life. When I tell people that I moved so many times growing up, they immediately assume that my dad was in the military. Nope, he just had what I have come to believe were several mid-life crises. He could never find his calling and was always trying to find his niche.

My father had been a very successful photocopier salesman at one point in his life. We moved to Anaheim into a brand-new house, just blocks from Disneyland. What more could a child want? That lasted two years. My dad would simply get bored with what he was doing, or it wouldn't give him the accolades that a he seemed to need. He was often looking for the road to becoming wealthy without doing the necessary work. When the riches didn't come, he'd move onto something else.

For me, having moved so times had its blessings and curses. Starting over is never easy for a young boy—going to a new school, trying to make new friends, and eating lunch alone way too many times. However, it did create a certain fortitude within me, where later in life I was able to not only survive my own life transitions, but to even flourish in them. Having had numerous transitions in life, I am constantly learning to depend more and more upon God, and less upon myself. I am learning to not make a permanent claim on the things of this world, because in this world things are always changing. As a friend has reminded me lately, there are no guarantees in this world. I am also learning that rather than focusing on my constantly changing circumstances, I need to focus on God's continual steadfastness, faithfulness, provision and guidance even in the wilderness—*his mercies are new every morning. Great is his faithfulness.*[40] We may not understand what is going on in a transition, but we can trust that God is in the midst of it, perhaps even allowing it to bring about his ultimate plan for our lives. As God says through the Prophet Jeremiah: "'I know the plans I have for you,' declares the Lord, 'plans to prosper you and not to harm you, plans to give you hope and a future.'"[41] During a transition, it can be hard

---

[40]    Lamentations 3.22-23 ESV
[41]    Jeremiah 29.11, NIV

to see or trust the plans of God. By now, at my age, after God's constant faithfulness, I thought I would have realized how much God has been with me throughout my entire life, even in all of my transitions. I am still learning. I keep being reminded, "The Lord your God has blessed you in all the work of your hands. He has watched over your journey through this vast wilderness. These forty years the Lord your God has been with you, and you have not lacked anything."[42]

These words were spoken to the Israelites as they were going through a transition, although be it a good transition, from slavery to freedom. However, it was a painful transition, a time of wandering in the desert, even though God had his eye upon them the whole time. For the Israelites, it was not just a time of transition or a year of transition; it was 40 years of transition. As great as the blessings can be during a transition, there is no denying the pain and grief of transitions. Any transition involves a letting go, a loss, and death of something that has been part of who we are, even if for just a brief time. I can't fault the Israelites for whining in the desert, wishing they had died back in Egypt. Remember, it was 40 years. Transitions, no matter what they are or how long they take, do not always feel good at the time.

The disciples also experienced a transition. They were with Jesus for a brief three years. In those three years, they experienced a lot and witnessed great and tragic events, all with someone who loved them in ways nobody ever could or would. Then, even though Jesus had prepared them for his impending death, they were lost when He eventually died. The death of any loved one is one of the most challenging transitions. However, any transition involves *death* of some kind. Something or someone is *dying* in the transition. Whatever we have lost in the transition will probably,

---

42    Deuteronomy 2.7, NIV

or even hopefully, be gone forever. Whatever it was that we had to die to during any transition was probably holding us back or weighing us down, preventing us from being who God had wanted us to be.

The blessing for the disciples was found three days after the Crucifixion at the Resurrection. In the meantime, they were perhaps sitting in their own personal tomb, cowered in a house, maybe sitting in the dark, numb and devastated but also afraid. Then, while the disciples were hiding behind locked doors, the Resurrected Christ appeared to them. The disciples were afraid, being unsure of what and who they were seeing. As Jesus enters the room, I can imagine the disciples huddling together, holding one another, shivering in fear, and moving away from Jesus as one big group, ending up in the corner of the room, not knowing what to do having nowhere to go.

In times of transition, in the now and not yet, you might be afraid. You may feel paralyzed, and unsure of what to do in the present, as you live between the past and the future. Like the disciples in Mark 6, you may feel you are in the middle of the lake, during a storm, between the shore you left behind and the shore you are trying to get to. You will become convinced that you will not make it to *the other side*, whatever *the other side* or *other shores* might be. You may think you have nothing left to give. You are afraid that you will be stuck in the *in-between* and never reach *the other side*.

After Jesus died and was buried, I'm sure the disciples felt as though they would not find *the other side*. The death of Jesus had put them into the middle of a transition that none expected. While their Savior was dead, they could not fathom what life would be like going forward. Yet, three days later, Jesus rose from the dead. Those were probably the longest three days for the disciples. Those three days were very dark and frightening for the disciples. They were in between what was and what was yet to come, but they could not imagine what was *yet to come*.

Jesus appears to the disciples in the upper room and says: "Peace be with you."[43] As Jesus spoke, as he breathed out the word *peace*, Scripture says the disciples received the Holy Spirit. It was as if the scales were removed from their eyes at that moment. Their grief, mixed with fear and confusion and hopelessness, subsided—at least for the moment.

God does the same for us during any earthly transition. He did that for me in another of my life transitions, between one job, career, ministry, and another. At the time, I had no idea what I would do next. I had just left a pastoral ministry without another job on the horizon. I was on a trapeze, letting go of the bar, only discovering there was nobody to catch me. I didn't know it at the time, but it was a transition. I was between the past and the future, the old and the new, the dying and the resurrection. I didn't know what the future held, but God did.

I had no idea how long it was going to last. There were no prospects, no hints of a new job, career, or ministry. It did not feel like a transition. It felt more like an ending than a new beginning. There was no *other side*. I didn't believe I had anything to offer anyone.

But then, while participating in a training session in Malaga, Spain— that's an entirely different story for another time—it's as if Jesus came into the room and said, "Peace." God used someone I just met to speak to me. During one session, sharing vulnerably about what I was going through, God spoke to me. I found myself speaking out loud what I heard, "God is not done with me." God still had a plan for me. There would be more transitions. more times of waiting on God, wondering what I would do. Those transitions became the crucibles for what God wanted to do in me, with me, and through me. In those times of transition, God shaped me and prepared me for what was yet to come.

---

43    John 20.19, NIV

In *Developing the Leader Within You*, John Maxwell, in the chapter 'Creating Positive Change,' describes how "most people are more comfortable with old problems than new solutions because the new represents the unknown." Maxwell quotes author and speaker Marilyn Ferguson, "it's not so much that we are afraid of change or so in love with the old ways, but it's that place in between that we fear… It's like being between trapezes. It's like being Linus when his blanket is in the dryer. There's nothing to hold on to."

I heard it said that people are not afraid of change but are afraid of transition. It's because the transition means that change is coming. It hasn't happened yet. And it's exactly that, the unknown future, that people do not like. Some platitudes are given, but they don't always help. The one saying that seems real and honest originated with Ann Lamott "when one door closes, another door opens… but it's hell in the hallway." Nobody likes being in the hallway.

However, it's in the hallway that God does some of his greatest work. It's in the transitions of life; even as we live in between the two advents of Christ, God does his greatest work. In seasons of transition, we feel adrift when the other side or the other shore does not appear on the horizon. God is at work doing a new thing, shaping and molding us to prepare us for what he knows is coming. So, don't rush through the transition—sit with what you are experiencing and feeling. Be present with the emotions that come to the surface. Those emotions are supposed to rise from within you, or else you aren't human; you aren't alive. Emotions are not bad. We serve a God who gave us those emotions. He, too, is filled with emotions, the greatest emotions being empathy and compassion. He understands our emotions. He is familiar with our suffering. So, don't deny your emotions, ignore them, or try to fix them—acknowledge them. Then, give them to the one who created you as an emotional being.

Ask God to replace grief with gladness, replace fear with peace, and replace despair with hope. As those emotions rise to the surface, they make room for what God wants to give you in their place—I will address that in *Part Two Releasing and Receiving*. Release to God whatever it is that keeps you paralyzed, stuck and afraid in whatever transition you are experiencing. Then, receive what God wants to give you as he prepares you for what only he knows is coming.

Let me end this chapter with a familiar story, re-told in many ways, including the Internet, from Cornelia Arnolda Johanna (*Corrie)* Ten Boom. Corrie is known for how her family helped Jewish people escape from the Nazis by hiding them in her home during World War II. I enjoyed a story about the dream that she told her sister Betsie. Corrie told her it was an *awful dream*. The dream woke Corrie up, filled with fear. She said to her sister,

> "I saw the Grote Market, half a block away, as clearly as though I were standing there, saw the town hall and St. Bavo's and the fish mart with its stair-stepped facade. Then as I watched, an odd, old farm wagon—old-fashioned and out of place in the middle of a city—came lumbering across the square pulled by four enormous black horses. To my surprise, I found that I was sitting in the wagon. And Father too! And Betsie! There were many others, some strangers, some friends. I recognized Pickwick and Toos, Willem and young Peter.
>
> All together, we were slowly being drawn across the square behind those horses. We couldn't get off the wagon, and that was the terrible thing. It was taking us away—far away, I felt—but we didn't want to go… Am I imagining

things because I am frightened? But it wasn't like that! It was real. Oh Betsie, was it a kind of vision?"

Betsie then replied, "I don't know. But if God has shown us bad times ahead, it's enough for me that he knows about them. That's why he sometimes shows us things, you know, to tell us that this too is in his hands."

We have no idea what lies ahead in a time or even a season of transition. We may imagine it to be *bad times ahead*. God may not show us what is coming as he did with Corrie Ten Boom. However, the truth and wisdom of Corrie's sister ring true for us that this is also *in his hands*. Whatever transition you are going through, as you grab the oars and strain towards whatever is coming next, not seeing, or sensing anything on the horizon, perhaps you need to put the oars down. Embrace the present, take your eyes off the future, engage with what God reveals, and trust and believe *that this too is in his hands.*

# Chapter 5

# OARS OF DEPRESSION

f you have ever been depressed, you will understand what I will write about in this chapter. If you have not been depressed, I hope this chapter will give you some insight into this very dark mental health disorder. If anything, it may help you recognize depression in the future, whether in yourself or somebody else.

Some people are depressed without even knowing it. They have been *straining at the oars*, trying to find joy and happiness, not knowing that they were suffering from depression. They just thought they were in a "funk". What I will share may help you recognize it and find hope to rise above it. I have realized that I may have been dealing with depression to some degree my whole life, even though the signs were there. In my younger years, depression was not something anybody talked about. I didn't understand what it was or that it even existed. When I was finally diagnosed with depression in my 40s, it all made sense. I even realized that my parents were depressed while I was growing up.

When people think about depression, they may have an image of Eeyore, the donkey friend of Winnie the Pooh. He walks around all day moaning and groaning about life. Would it surprise you if I said I think Tigger is also an image of depression? My depression played out more like Tigger than Eeyore. I know, it doesn't make sense. Tigger seems so full of life, energetic, and enthusiastic. He seems to enjoy every day, hopping around everywhere he goes and exhibiting that funny laugh. You would not suspect him of depression. Just to be clear, I am not a psychiatrist. I am not seriously trying to diagnose Eeyore or Tigger as having depression. *Humor me a bit—I realize that Eeyore and Tigger are cartoon characters.* I am trying to say that it is hard to spot what depression looks like in someone unless you have experienced depression, like me.

People who knew me as I was growing up would say I was more like Tigger—energetic, outgoing, humorous, and maybe even the life of the party. They didn't know—what I didn't fully know—I was that way to cover up my insecurity and lack of confidence, which was probably a low level of depression. My outward behavior and appearance were not always reflections of what was inside me. I was constantly comparing myself negatively with everyone else. I was part of the *in-crowd*, but I always felt like I was on the outside. That's not always what causes depression, but it can be how depression makes itself known. I was never happy with who I was. I never felt good enough. I presented myself as confident, happy, and full of energy, but trying to keep up that persona was exhausting. If I was ever *down*, people thought something was wrong. The truth was, there was something wrong. Yes, I'm an introvert, but that is not necessarily what causes depression. As an introvert, I had to work at being an extrovert that seemed natural to everyone else. They didn't know it was all a *show*. I was covering up that I was not comfortable or happy with who I was deep down inside, and I didn't want anyone to know it.

I have this other picture of me growing up. It's the one of a duck on the water. You probably know where I'm going with this. On the surface, a duck looks like they are having a jolly good old time, calmly moving about in the water with little effort, as if they are gliding above the surface. Below the surface, their webbed feet are scrambling hard to move just a little bit at a time. For people who knew me, it probably looked like I had things all together like the duck. Yet, below the surface, there was a lot of chaos. People are surprised when I tell them that I am an introvert. That's because most people do not know the true definition of an introvert versus an extrovert.

Let me take a little sidestep here and point out what I mean when I use *extrovert* and *introvert*. Typically, people think of an extrovert as a Tigger. Extroverts are energetic, bouncing all over the place, happy with life. Nothing seems to get them down. On the other hand, people think of an introvert as quiet, maybe even shy, a recluse. There is nothing wrong with those descriptions. However, an extrovert needs to be around people and feed off people. They like to be with energetic people because they get filled up. So, yes, they also look like energetic people.

On the other hand, an introvert gets filled up by being alone and spending time in quiet and stillness. It's not as though an introvert cannot have a good time or be around energetic people, but doing so for too long drains them, and they need time alone. That was me, and to a degree, it still is me. I get energized by doing what I am doing right now; sitting by myself in a coffee shop and writing or reading. The odd part is that what I love about being in a coffee shop is all the people around me, but they don't need anything from me.

Now that you know a little bit about me and my battle with depression, perhaps you can understand why it seemed as though I was constantly *straining at the oars* to make people like me. I was not acting like an extrovert for any other reason than I believed that what people wanted from me was what they needed. I couldn't act any differently. If I was not constantly outgoing, I was afraid people would get to know the real me, the me that I knew, the me that I didn't like, and they would stop liking me. That became too exhausting. The truth that I have come to know and has set me free is that I cannot please everybody, and I cannot make everybody like me. It is not my job to do either. I also didn't know that all my effort was to please people or be liked by them. With the help of counseling and medication, I have accepted who I am. I have come to accept myself, the person who God has created me to be and who I am becoming. As one who always seeks the approval and acceptance of others, I am learning that God is my number one fan. Again, it's an ongoing learning process. I still have moments when depression raises its ugly head. However, I'm starting to recognize it and not allow it to debilitate me. I'm also learning how to be more honest about it with people who truly care about me.

The effect of COVID-19, the lockdowns, and having to work from home allowed people like me to be in their happy place. It made the extroverts go crazy as they needed to be around people, but they could not do so. I may be an introvert, but I must be an extrovert for my ministry. Some of my most exhausting days are Sunday mornings. When I get home, I sit down, put my feet up, take a deep breath, and before I know it, I am fast asleep. Most people do that on Sunday afternoons, falling asleep while watching football. That doesn't mean they are introverts exhausted from being an extrovert. So, I can be an extrovert, but I have also realized that I operate covertly as an introvert, even in crowds. I can be a great host, making sure everybody is cared for, while not engaging myself in an extended conversation with anyone. I may even get people to participate in a game that I don't have to participate in because I'm leading the game. They all have to do something together in the game—not me. When speaking to a crowd, I will often have them get into small groups to discuss matters—I don't have to be in a group. I head for the bathroom if I'm at a meeting or somewhere else and the leader or speaker wants us to get into small groups.

I can stay true to who I am as an introvert while in a crowd of people by not staying in one place too long. I can hang out with one crowd for a little, with my skin crawling as I look for a way to escape. I can then bop over to another group, nod my head a bit, laugh, and move on, even if I don't understand the joke someone just said. Being with many people at one time does not always fill me up. I am much better off sitting on a couch and having a conversation with just one other person. That's not how most people saw me.

I can remember people asking me occasionally if everything was alright. I assured them I was fine. However, they were concerned because I was so quiet. It wasn't that I was quiet all day or for days. Something was surely wrong if I wasn't energetic, humorous, fully engaged in conversations, and reserved. Nothing was wrong, necessarily. I was just me, the real me. Yet, something was wrong. I was exhausted. I was depressed. I just didn't know it. I thought I was quiet, having a bad day, or not feeling great. I knew there was more going on because I couldn't shake it. I couldn't just flip a switch and be energetic.

Part of my personality was a driving force to prove myself to others. I remember going through ordination and being told that *you will never be a scholar, but you will make a good pastor.* I took it to mean that to be a scholar is greater than being just a pastor. Fortunately, although I didn't appreciate or accept what this group of strangers told me, they were right—I have been a good pastor. I am only now accepting that is who I am, and that is enough. Being a *good pastor* is who I am, and that's a good thing. Unfortunately, I spent a lot of time and energy trying to become a scholar. I wanted to prove to them, but more importantly, prove to myself that they were wrong. To this day, I do not consider myself a scholar—thank God.

God has called me to be a pastor—a good pastor. That is what I am and always will be.

However, I never felt that I was good enough at whatever I was doing. The worst part is that I believed that everybody else thought the same thing about me. I could preach a sermon, be given words of encouragement, but feeling terrible about the sermon myself. I kept telling myself, *well, I will do better next week.* I now believe that was all part of my depression. I never felt competent. I was always concerned about what others thought about what I was doing. A friend of mine once helped me with those battles. He said to me, "Bill, people are not sitting around talking about you all the time." What? Of course, they were. They talked about how terrible the youth group was or how boring my last sermon was. Of course, they are talking about me. *Great, I'm also a narcissist. I will cover that personality type later.*

So, why am I sharing all this personal information with you? Because I gave the appearance of being energetic, the life of the party, and having it all together. It was keeping me from dealing with the deep waters of depression that I believe I have experienced my entire life. Don't get me wrong. I did not look or act depressed all the time, but I can look back and recognize certain times, behaviors, and attitudes as signs of my depression. I honestly don't know which came first. Was I an extrovert trying to overcompensate for and cover up the reality that I was an introvert that eventually led to depression? Or was it depression that kept me from accepting who I was and being happy with myself? Depression can be the result of a variety of things. Mostly, it's a chemical imbalance, one that can go undiagnosed for a long time.

Depression can also manifest itself differently for each person. For me it was the lack of joy, motivation, energy, or even an appetite. I would sleep a lot—I mean a lot. For others, depression can show itself in uncharacteristic anger, which was part of my issue as well. Depression can cause anxiety and fear. A traumatic event can trigger something within a person that leads to depression. For some there is no sense of hope for the future as panic sets in. Some people, without really knowing it, find themselves being busier than normal, almost frantic about things. There is not a simple understanding about where depression comes from, or how it manifests itself.

As life went on, I would hit some patches where I felt a bit blue, a bit *off*, or what I would say was a *funk*. "What's going on with you? You seem out of it." "Oh, I'm just in a funk." This went on for years. In my 40's I eventually sought out a counselor. He told me that I was probably dealing with depression, and that I had probably been functioning with a low level of depression my whole life. I soon saw a psychiatrist, which was hard to accept and admit. Only crazy people see a psychiatrist, or so I thought. The psychiatrist help me understand that having depression meant that my brain was not operating on all cylinders. This news was so helpful and liberating for me. I wasn't crazy. Well, at least not clinically. Fortunately, with ongoing counseling and even some medications, I have been able to manage my depression more consistently.

While not operating on all cylinders I didn't realize I had been *straining At the oars* of depression while striving to be an extrovert, wanting to well-liked and even applauded, as though that would make me happier. I would, and perhaps still do, compare myself to others. I was a bit paranoid, okay, highly paranoid, about what other people were saying or thinking about me because it was undoubtedly negative. I believed in the lie that I was not good enough. (Yeah, daddy issues.) Lauren Daigle's *song You Say* has been a theme for me the past few years.

Part of the song says, "*I keep fighting voices in my mind that say I'm not enough. Every single lie that tells me I will never measure up.*" (Read the rest of the lyrics sometime—I'm too busy trying to meet my deadline this week so that my book writing coach is happy with me.)

I used to tell myself that I was not competent, capable, worthy, or even adequate. I was below average. It turns out I'm just average. I'm like so many other people. Maybe even you. Struggling with depression has given me greater empathy for people experiencing what I went through. It has developed within me an awareness of people who may be depressed or have signs of depression—I can see it in their eyes. I told a friend of mine who was battling depression, shocked to hear my own story, that *nobody gets it until you get it.* Most people cannot comprehend what it is feels like to experience depression, until, sadly, they too experience depression.

My experience of depression has opened doors of ministry, allowing me to help others navigate the deep waters of depression. People with depression believe they are the only ones suffering and that no one can relate to them. I thought no one but me had ever experienced depression. Fortunately, one Saturday morning, a friend invited me to breakfast—he had heard about my depression. He was my age, a very successful surgeon, and recently married. He looked like he had it all together. As we talked and I shared what was going on, I thought he was listening to me as a doctor—that was not true—he shared with me about his own battle with depression. I was shocked. There was no way he had ever been depressed. I looked at him in disbelief and remember saying, "But, you're ok now?" I will never forget what he said, "Yes, and you will be too. You will get through this." That gave me hope.

I am by no means an expert when it comes to depression. I am not a psychiatrist or a counselor. I share only what I have personally experienced, and from what I have learned over the years. If you are wondering whether or not you have depression, you might need to find help. You may simply need to grab breakfast with someone who has been where you are, hear their testimony, and know that you too will get through this. It may be time you sought professional help. There's nothing wrong with seeing a professional who can help you navigate these deep and dark waters. If that is where you find yourself right now, stop reading this book, pick up the phone, call a friend, or a pastor, someone who can lead you to a good counselor of psychiatrist. Don't put it off.

# Chapter 6

# OARS OF NARCISSISM

**A**s much as I loved body surfing and boogie boarding, I also feared the ocean. The undertow that had taken the life of a friend was always at the back of my mind. I can spot an undertow most of the time. As the waves come crashing onto the shore, there is a lot of sand that begins to kick up from the bottom, where the undertow is beginning to take shape, with a strong pull that takes even the strongest of swimmers out further into the ocean. It makes it hard, if not impossible, to swim back to the shore. Try swimming against the undertow, and it's like *straining at the oars*. Instead of making *headway painfully*, you are not making any headway. It's futile. Keep trying to swim against the undertow, and it will eventually exhaust you to the point where you can no longer stay above water. The undertow then carries you out to sea. What you must do once you recognize you are in the undertow, is to start horizontal to the shoreline until you are out of the grip of the undertow. You will never make it to shore if you try swimming against the undertow. It's too strong.

The image of that undertow is how it feels to live with a narcissist. You keep trying to get out of their grip, break the cycle, and stop the dance, but they continue to bait you, lure you into their trap, and prevent you from getting away. Narcissism, is a fairly new concept for me. To be honest, everyone has probably encountered difficult relationships without realizing that they were dealing with a narcissist. They keep thinking things will change, but the reality is that a narcissist will usually never change. It's hard to admit that you are in a relationship with a narcissist. It's even harder to admit that you might be the problem. Yes, you may have narcissistic tendencies that make it hard to have healthy relationships. I admit that I certainly do have narcissistic tendencies that keep me *straining at the oars* in certain relationships. What I have learned is that whenever I encounter a narcissist, their behavior often brings out my own narcissistic behavior. It's a no win situation. The biggest narcissistic trait I have seen raise its ugly head in me, is the need to always be right. It's hard to admit that I am wrong. Hopefully I am getting better.

What became apparent to me through counseling, is that I grew up with a narcissist dad. However, like depression, the term narcissist was not used much when I was growing up. In fact, my counselor helped me acknowledge that my was and is a *wounded narcissist*. More than likely, his narcissistic tendencies came from his being wounded himself by other narcissists in his life. I cannot say with any authority that my dad is a narcissist or even a *wounded narcissist*. However, as I have done some reading on the subject, the signs are there. I love my dad and have been able to take responsibility for myself, without blaming him for my own faults. I have even been able to forgive him for some of what he did that left scars on me. I do not want to play the victim here. I just want to hopefully share what I have learned about the difficulties of being in a relationship with a narcissist.

One of the hardest lessons for me has been accepting the fact that I have been in relationships with narcissists throughout my life. It seems to judgmental. However, admitting the truth has helped me come to realize that I am not always the problem in any given relationship. Narcissists have a way of convincing me that it is all about me. I am the one with issues, not them. Over the years I was convinced that I was always wrong (maybe that's why I hate being wrong), and that I was the one who had to do better in the relationship.

With my dad, it was about me having to be a better son. It was never about him having to be a better dad. Being in a relationship like that is an exhausting way to live. Little did I know that I was *straining at the oars* trying to please my dad, which was never going to possible. Even as an adult I have struggled to not allow my dad's narcissistic tactics derail me or suck me in like an undertow. Narcissists have a way of sucking you into their madness, either by once again convincing you that you are wrong, or causing you to erupt with anger trying to defeat them by defending yourself. I admit, I have seen myself become like my dad, and it never accomplishes anything. For way too long I kept giving my dad another chance, only to discover he was not going to change. Each time it was like trying to against an undertow. I thought for sure things would be different next time. (Remember the definition of insanity?)

As hard as it seemed at the time, I eventually had to separate myself from my dad, physically and emotionally. Still, even today, after years of distancing myself from him, sensing it might be save to get back in the water, I will occasionally answer his phone call. Every time I immediately get sucked into the undertow of his narcissism. I have learned that it is not safe to go back into the water yet. I don't ignore him completely, but I do not engage as much as he wants me to.

Maybe you have been *straining at the oars* in a significant relationship, and you find yourself wondering why it's so difficult. You feel exhausted because you can never seem to please the other person or persons. Maybe you don't know why you keep developing relationships with such difficult people. They may not be narcissists, but they might have narcissistic tendencies. And, guess what? If you grew up with a narcissist, more than likely you drift towards what you are familiar with. It's hard to spot a narcissist, but there are some signs that I have learned about. However, like with an undertow, you may not realize you are dealing with a narcissist at the beginning. But, before you know it, the undertow is beating you up and dragging you down.

Let me share a little bit of what I have learned about narcissists. Again, I am not the expert, but have learned a lot by experience. You may want to do so me researching on your own, rather than just taking my word for it. One of the things I have learned is that narcissists have an inflated sense of self-importance. They don't even realize it, even though others can see it. With a narcissist there is an excessive interest in, or admiration of, oneself and one's physical appearance. Narcissists also have a deep need for excessive attention and admiration. In addition, they have troubled relationships that often are a result of their having a lack of empathy for others. Why would they? The relationship is all about them. If the relationship no longer meets their needs or benefits them, they are quick to walk away and find someone else who will be their "supplier". I think of it as feeding their ego.

On *Quora*—a social question and answer website—someone wrote that a narcissist needs constant validation. Again, if someone is not supplying that validation, they will go find someone who will. Narcissists are very fragile individuals. They need people to not only like them, but to basically worship them. A narcissist must persuade someone to like them, to the point that the other person suppresses your desires, needs, goals, and aspirations in order to please the narcissist. More than that, a narcissist wants the other person to see them as grandiose as they seem themselves. Are any lights going on for you right now? Do you find yourself smiling a bit, nodding your head because the name of somebody you know came to mind? You might even be wondering if you are a narcissist. In fact, as I read about narcissists, I wondered if I truly was the problem. The truth is, we all have narcissistic tendencies, but it doesn't mean we are a narcissist.

If any of the above defines you more than you like to admit, perhaps you need to put down the book, find someone who can help process what you might be discovering about yourself. If you are beginning to consider that you may be working with, or even living with a narcissist, you also may want to get some help to learn how to either live with them or how to possibly walk away from the relationship. I pray that you can be set you free from the lies you may have been telling yourself. The truth is this: It is not all about you, and it is not all your fault. If you can embrace that truth, my guess is that you are not a narcissist. A narcissist believes it is all about them, and that whatever is wrong, it is all your fault.

Narcissism is not new. We have Adam and Eve to thank for this rather confusing personality disorder. Or, we can blame original sin. If that is true, it still doesn't excuse any of our narcissistic behaviors. Even if Adam and Eve were not narcissistic, they at least had a very self-centered and perhaps inflated view of who they were and could be, even to the point of disobeying God. Plus, when the truth was found out, neither of them could take blame. It was the other person's fault, including the serpent.

Original sin begins with the self-centeredness that lies within all of us. IF it goes unchecked, it can turn into narcissism.

I also discovered that narcissism is found in a lot of the people we know in the Bible. You don't have to go very far in the Old Testament before you come to the person of Saul. He would do anything to eliminate someone trying to be superior to himself—David. He went on a warpath trying to kill David, eliminating his competition. Then, in the New Testament, King Herod was not about to let some baby, the one called "King of the Jews", strip him of his power. Herod's self-inflated sense of importance caused him to order the death of all first-born male infants, which would surely get rid of baby Jesus. No baby was going to rob Herod of what he believed was his rightful throne and the admiration of the people. Fortunately, God had other plans.

When I considered Jesus and the 12 disciples, I wondered if the brothers James and John were a bit narcissistic—and their mother didn't help. There were times when Jesus would share with the disciples about his impending death. He was not soliciting pity or wanting anyone to defend him, although Peter was dead set against Jesus dying. Jesus was preparing them for the inevitable. After being with Jesus for three years, there was soon a time when the disciples would no longer have him around. That was pretty heavy stuff. Jesus was bearing his soul.

One such incident came as the disciples and Jesus were traveling to Jerusalem. Jesus took the 12 aside. In Mark's account, the conversation went, "We are going up to Jerusalem," he said, "and the Son of Man will be delivered over to the chief priests and the teachers of the law. They will condemn him to death and will hand him over to the Gentiles, who will mock him and spit on him, flog him and kill him. Three days later he will rise."[44] In response to what Jesus said, which was very deep and personal, I believe James and John, perhaps without missing a beat, showed their narcissistic tendencies. And it runs in the family. After Jesus tells them this horrific news, James and John respond by saying: *Teacher, we want you to do for us whatever we ask.* That is the definition of a narcissist. *I referred to this moment earlier about* drinking the cup. Narcissists want others to do whatever it is that will continue to feed and inflate their sense of importance or their need to be in control. Also, like any narcissist, James and John did not

---

[44]    Mark 10.33-34, NIV

possess any empathy for Jesus. Jesus shared the grief he was experiencing with the disciples as he contemplated his impending death. How did James and John respond? "Let one of us sit at your right and the other at your left in your glory." Narcissistic? Self-centered? Lack of empathy? I'm just saying. James and John had no idea what they were asking Jesus to do or how self-centered they were being. What were the other disciples thinking about this very unusual behavior by James and John? Was it typical behavior of James and John?

Interestingly, Matthew has a different record of that same event. Jesus, again, is traveling to Jerusalem with the disciples. He pulls them aside and tells them about what is going to happen. But this time, it is the mother of James and John who gets involved. *The apple doesn't fall far from the tree.* Two questions come to mind. Did the sons grow up with a narcissistic mom? It's hard to tell. We don't know much about her. Or was the mom enabling her two narcissistic sons? I'm going to put my money on the latter.

Narcissists will not change if those around them, particularly those in their family, continue to enable their behavior. That is part of the *straining at the oars* when living with a narcissist. The narcissist's world has been working for them, and those who live with them or are associated with them keep helping make their world work for them without knowing it. Those of us who lived with a narcissist didn't know that we were helping promote their unhealthy behavior by doing their bidding. I enabled my dad's behavior unwittingly and unknowingly, but still, I did not break the cycle. When my dad said *jump,* I did not question why he wanted me to jump. I just jumped. He was my dad. After all, dads are always in charge. Dads are always right. Or at least that's what I grew up believing in our household.

I've also learned that you don't question a narcissist. You just jump and keep on jumping. Why? Because what I also learned is that when you do jump, it is never enough. No matter how good you are, you are never good enough. So, obviously you can jump higher, until you're done jumping. Ok, it isn't literally about jumping. You get the point.

I do remember one time, when I was about 16 years old, I got the courage to ask my dad if I could talk to him about something he did to me that hurt. He was very gracious as he sat and listened to me. Wow. What an incredible experience. That was until I was done talking. Throughout the whole time I was talking, my dad truly seemed to be listening. He even was nodding his head as though he understood me. In the end, he asked, "Are you done?" I was done alright. I had said what I wanted to say. It felt good. Then it happened. Without hardly a beat, my dad said, "Let me tell you where you're wrong." I honestly don't remember what happened next. If you experience being around a narcissist, you know that you are always wrong, which means they are never wrong. I can't recall my dad ever saying he was wrong or apologizing for anything. Maybe it happened. Maybe I'm selling him short. Maybe I'm wrong—darn it, I'm still in his trap.

Something else I learned in a post written by Psychologist Elinor Greenberg, is what she calls the difference between *Black Knight Narcissists* and *White Knight Narcissists.* Greenberg writes,

> "Black Knight Narcissists get their narcissistic supplies from sadistically setting out to demolish other people's self-esteem and pleasure in life. White Knights are still Narcissists, despite their desire to be seen as helpful, generous, and kind. White Knight Narcissists get their narcissistic supplies from doing good deeds and being seen as great human beings. The reality is that doing good deeds is just another way for them to seize the spotlight and shore up their shaky self-esteem. Having said that, I

still recognize that many of us have benefited from White Knight Narcissists' need to be seen as special and that this is preferable than them actively wanting to harm other people."

Greenberg lists the following characteristics of *White Knight Narcissists*:

- They want you to think they are good people.
- They will do favors for other people that make them look good.
- If they are wealthy, they are likely to be philanthropists who give away large sums of money to causes they support—as long as they get public recognition for doing so.
- Some are *good neighbor narcissists*. This means they will offer to pick up groceries for sick neighbors, help someone put up their window screens, or do another chore.
- Helping people makes them feel important and enhances their self-esteem.

It is hard to be angry, critical, or judgmental about a *White Knight Narcissist*. The hardest part is that for those who don't live with them, the *White Knight Narcissist* appears to be such a kind and humble, and most serving person. What draws a person to a *White Knight Narcissist* is what will become less attractive as they are more loving and generous to others than the person who is perhaps now married to them. Greenberg explains that once a *White Knight Narcissist* is married, their need to be supplied by strangers causes them to no longer be loving, generous, and kind to their spouse. Their spouse has already supplied them with enough, so they search for another supplier who could turn out to be a neighbor. If the marriage falls apart, the neighbor cannot understand how the spouse of the *White*

*Knight Narcissist* could find any fault with such a kind, loving and generous person.

The deception of a charming and outgoing narcissist, is that they truly believe they are always right, know more than anybody else in the room and use that to be the center of attention. They are so convincing and can pull the wool over everyone's eyes. In public, my dad was a charmer, and people loved him. However, he was a con man, a salesman, and he would get you, hook, line, and sinker every time. Even if you struggled with believing what he was saying, he could be so convincing that you began to doubt what you knew to be true. Yep, that's what a narcissist does. They make you second guess yourself. They are passionate, opinionated, the brightest bulb in the room, or so they think, and everyone else feels so dim and dark and insignificant. You dare not question anything they say. You get caught in their web, and they slowly lure you in, and you find yourself *straining at the oars* to get away, but it's futile. It took me years to realize that my dad wasn't always right. I discovered that he often lied or exaggerated the truth, all in an attempt to build himself up in the eyes of others. My brother and sister took a little longer to realize the tangled web they were in. It's not their fault. Somehow, our dad had us believing that we were nothing without him. Our dad wanted us all to be dependent upon him. He wanted us to need him. A narcissist needs people to need them. They also need to be wanted.

Again, I am not the expert on narcissists. I am not the one who can tell you what to do if you are in a relationship with a narcissist. I share all of this because perhaps you may be wondering why you are in a relationship that seems as though you are incapable of doing anything right. You have been *straining at the oars* for a long time, wondering why it seems as though you're the only one contributing, and are tired of walking on eggshells around a certain person. You are convinced that you are doing something wrong. You are questioning why you cannot make the other person happy, or why they are so unsatisfied with what you are doing. Yet, you are still in the relationship.

I won't pretend I have any answers but let me share the signs and symptoms of a narcissistic personality disorder I found on the Mayo Clinic website. Perhaps the light will go on for you, and you can begin to learn how to live with a narcissist or determine that it's time you can no longer do so, and may need to walk away, at least temporarily.

The severity of symptoms can vary, although people with a narcissistic personality disorder can:

- have an exaggerated sense of self-importance,
- have a sense of entitlement and require constant excessive admiration,
- expect to be recognized as superior even without achievements that warrant it,
- exaggerate achievements and talents,
- be preoccupied with fantasies about success, power, brilliance, beauty, or the perfect mate,
- believe they are superior and can only associate with equally special people,
- monopolize conversations and belittle or look down on people they perceive as inferior,
- expect special favors and unquestioning compliance with their expectations,
- take advantage of others to get what they want,
- have an inability or unwillingness to recognize the needs and feelings of others,
- be envious of others and believe others envy them,

- behave arrogantly or haughtily, coming across as arrogant, boastful, and pretentious,
- insist on having the best of everything—for instance, the best car of office.

At the same time, people with a narcissistic personality disorder have trouble handling anything they perceive as criticism, and they can:

- become impatient or angry when they don't receive special treatment,
- have significant interpersonal problems and easily feel slighted,
- react with rage or contempt and try to belittle the other person to make themselves appear superior,
- have difficulty regulating emotions and behavior,
- experience major problems dealing with stress and adapting to change,
- feel depressed and moody because they fall short of perfection,
- have secret feelings of insecurity, shame, vulnerability, and humiliation.

I don't know how many symptoms a person needs to be classified as a narcissist or to have a narcissistic personality disorder. Remember, we can probably see a bit of ourselves in these descriptions. If we are healthy enough, we can identify our narcissistic tendencies and get help to overcome them. I can certainly see myself in some of the above. I wonder if my issues result from growing up with a narcissist.

I believe that God's grace and his divine appointment in other relationships have kept me from falling into the narcissistic abyss. That's not to say I'm perfect. I have my moments—we all do. It's about how quickly we overcome our mistakes before we cause too much damage to others.

It wasn't so much spotting the signs of a narcissist that caused me to seek help. It was paying attention to my unhealthy reactions and behaviors around a narcissist that made me realize I was caught in the undercurrent of narcissism. In a counseling session, I was introduced to FOG, an acronym for Fear Obligation Guilt. Those three words describe how most people respond to a narcissist. In my relationship with my father, I checked all the boxes. I was always afraid of being punished, not doing the right things, being scolded, and even being given a whipping with a belt. So, I lived to keep the peace, please my dad, and gain his approval to escape wrath, disappointment, anger, and disapproval. If I didn't make him happy, I felt bad. I was a bad person, a bad son, which led to living in response to a narcissist out of obligation. I had to live according to what he thought a good son should do with my dad. I was even told to help my brother out at one point by giving him some money. My dad would pay me back, but he didn't want my brother to know it came from him. When I said I didn't want to lie to my brother about the money, my dad said, "Your brother needs a father right now." *Of course, if I brought that up to my dad today, he would deny it ever happened—something he has done in the past.* My dad was trying to make me feel obligated to be the *father* or the *older brother*—it was pure manipulation. Which then creates the final response—Guilt. If I didn't do what my father said I should do, he would try to convince me to do it by making me feel guilty. Even to the point where if I didn't do what he wanted me to do, he would say, "You're no son of mine."

Living in a FOG is oppressing, especially when you don't realize it at the time. I could have saved myself a lot of heartache, energy, and pain if I knew I was living with a narcissist or what they even meant. I would not have felt guilty about not being good enough. Living with a narcissist eroded my self-confidence, made me question who I was and caused me to have doubts about what I could do. If I had known what I know now, I would have saved time and energy seeing a counselor. I could have stopped the dance long ago if I had known what was happening. Ok—maybe not.

When you are in a relationship with a narcissist, you will be *straining at the oars* and making little if no progress. It may take years to realize it, and by the time you do, it could be that you have no more energy to try to save the relationship. At some point, you have to put down the oars of Fear, Obligation, and Guilt that keep you from moving forward.

## Chapter 7

# OARS OF CONFLICT

Conflict can bring about the best and the worst in people. Part of the problem with conflict is that most people do not like conflict. They avoid conflict. Yes, I'm speaking for myself, but admit it, conflict is not fun. I believe that part of the reason people do not like conflict is because they are poor at confrontation. I believe that people do not like conflict and avoid confrontation because they do not necessarily possess healthy communication skills or have been hurt by conflict in the past. When someone has been hurt or wounded, it may be because the conflict was not handled well or because the confrontation was not done with a motive of genuine love or from a place of compassion or empathy. The truth is we have all been wounded by past conflicts and confrontations that did not end well due to a lack of healthy communication skills and boundaries.

That being said, it is true that *wounded people wound people.* Or *hurt people hurt people.* We inflict pain on others because we have experienced a lot of pain ourselves. Unfortunately, an old playground taunt is not true. You know the one, *sticks and stones may break my bones, but words will never hurt me.* Seriously? I'd rather withstand being pelted with sticks and stones than by hurtful words. Hurtful words have inflicted longer-lasting pain to my heart, soul, and mind than anything that could harm me physically.

There's a saying I have heard many times, *death by a million paper cuts.*

Have you ever had a paper cut? It's the tiniest of cuts, but it inflicts great pain. Once the pain subsides, the irritation of the wound is still there. I cannot imagine having *a million* paper cuts. Of course, it is an overstatement. The saying refers to what is repeatedly inflicted on us that wounds us more than any single swipe of a giant sword. The little words that have been hurled at us, intentionally or not, or even passive-aggressively, hurt tremendously. It could be the whispers of others that are filled with gossip and rumors about you, inflict that inflict you in ways you may never even know. Sometimes the afflictions keep on coming, as though we are just one big red bullseye or a magnet that draws all the afflictions in our direction. We resolve one issue, or perhaps just put a band-aid on it until more can be done when another barrage of verbal affliction comes against us.

It can seem like waves at the ocean coming against us, knocking us down, only to have another one crash upon us as we struggle to get up. I loved going out into the ocean and body surfing or boogie boarding. However, in order to catch a good wave, I had to get out beyond the waves crashing on the shore. I had to get out to where the waves first began swelling. There were times when I would be walking out into the water only to keep getting knocked back by wave after wave. It was hard to make any progress. The waves just keep on coming. I vividly remember being at the beach as a teenager, trying to get out into the ocean. The waves were coming in so fast and from every direction imaginable that it was near impossible. The waves were crisscrossing each other. At some point, I had to stop trying. It's too exhausting. I was not making any *headway.*

Seven months into the COVID-19 pandemic, there was additional ongoing tension in our country due to violence, police brutality, and racism. There were also raging fires and hurricanes and a tumultuous presidential election. The battle lines seemed to become more and more apparent. The divisions in our country, in families, in churches, and between friends became ever more apparent. Oh, the divisions were already there. During the pandemic they were just being exposed in an ugly and painful manner. On top of the pandemic, our country began to experience all kinds of conflict, resulting in violence and anger as people found new ways to be judgmental, critical, and even downright rude and nasty. People became unhinged because they had to wear a mask or because someone wasn't wearing a mask. People were assaulted verbally and physically.

I witnessed individuals lose their patience on a zoom call. They acted with such a rage nobody saw coming, or even knew existed, or that they were capable of displaying such hostile emotions. I heard adults discuss how their older parents became angry and bitter as they lived isolated from family and friends or just society itself. Who could blame them. Other pastors shared with me how members in their church wrote them hurtful letters, pledging never to attend their church again, kicking dirt as they left, making it known how angry they were at the church, the pastor, and the leaders. *I was secretly praying those people didn't come to our church.* Pastors shared how church members were angry because their church was not opening like the ones down the street or because they had opened when they didn't believe it should. The church I was serving had similar experiences, but not to the extent some pastors friends encountered. It was as if you could not win.

Something I read during the pandemic gave some helpful advice. First, make plans, but stay flexible. Second, hope for good things, but not expect anything. Every plan I made was done with a sense of caution. Seminary did not teach me about how to handle a pandemic. I was wanting to be sensitive to everyone involved in making plans, as well as those who would be affected by those plans. It was not a matter of pleasing people, but I knew we couldn't please everyone. It was a matter of prayer and Godly wisdom from others, as well as paying attention to what was being dictated by any local officials. Those of us involved in making plans one day, knew they could be changed the next. It was a huge learning curve for everyone, and it became very exhausting trying to navigate the turbulent waters. A lot of time and energy was spent on making decisions that, in the end, had to be scrapped. Sometimes it was due to the ongoing changing situations our country and our world were experiencing. It was due to the changing protocols in our city, county, and state. One day we are in phase 2, and the next, we're back into phase 1. It's this uncertainty, the roller coaster of decisions being made, that I have no doubt added to the various volatile reactions. People were experiencing a lot of stress and anxiety.

I remember in the '90s how youth leaders were saying how that particular generation of teenagers was the most stressed-out generation ever. This was due to what experts were saying was a lack of consistency in their lives. Nothing ever stayed the same. It was as if the land they were standing on was constantly shifting. Whenever they stepped onto something they thought was secure and stable, they quickly had to jump to another spot because of the changing landscape of the day. The stress experienced is comparable to trying to cross a freeway without getting hit by a car or a truck.

Some of it in the 90's was due to the rapid change in technology and entertainment. Young people became bored with the latest creation and looked for the next big thing. Since then, I believe that constant change has become a way of life for *today's youth*. Change, transitions, and adapting to circumstances are all they know. That kind of instability and lack of consistency can create angst within anybody, but particularly youth. I recently heard a lecture by Dr Kara Powell, Executive Director of the Fuller Youth Institute. In her new book, *3 Big Questions That Change Every Teenager,* Powell explains how "today's teenagers are the most anxious, adaptive, and diverse generation in history, which can make it hard for us to relate." Dr Powell describes how teenagers today ask three questions: Who am I? Where do I fit? What difference can I make? It makes me wonder if today's generation will remain in any lengthy relationship, stay at a job until retirement, or live in one house their entire life. With so much changing in their lives, anything that seems permanent may cause them to grow restless. They may not know how to accept something long enough to see it through to the end. When the going gets tough, they just move on to something or someone else.

That is what often happens in times of conflict. Rather than face it head-on, working through the issues, it seems easier just to cut ties and move on. Something has changed in the relationship, and it's much easier just to walk away. Sometimes it be necessary, as I mentioned when dealing with a narcissist. However, as I learned years ago, even if you leave a church, or a relationship when conflict arises, wherever you go, you are still there. And believe it or not, you can't run away from yourself. You are part of the problem. You are part of the conflict. Rather than being part of the solution, you take your own set of problems somewhere else until the next conflict. If you have found this to be true, that conflict tends to follow you wherever you go, you may need to look within yourself.

So, where does conflict come from? From within us, or, should I say, from within you. Consider the following, "What causes fights and quarrels among you? Don't they come from your desires that battle within you? You desire but do not have, so you kill. You covet but you cannot get what you want, so you quarrel and fight. You do not have because you do not ask God. When you ask, you do not receive, because you ask with wrong motives, that you may spend what you get on your pleasures."[45]

We all must take time to understand why we tend to run into conflict or why we run from conflict. We all need to understand why, when conflict comes, we tend to grab our oars tightly without even realizing it. You'll know when it happens if you pay attention to your inner self, the feelings, blood pressure, anxiety, and heart beating faster. I don't think anybody likes conflict. Even more than that, I believe most people, myself included, don't know how to handle conflict.

I have considered how much conflict can cause us to pick up our oars and begin frantically trying to row, perhaps wanting to avoid it altogether. I have realized that perhaps we strain and struggle with conflict because of our flawed human nature that sees everything as a competition. So many people are out for their own personal gain. It's what is being communicated and celebrated these days. The culture of *me, myself, and I* has been around a long time, but it has created a sense of entitlement these days. So many people are convinced they are the center of the universe and entitled to have life on their terms. In a society where bad behavior and competition are normal, those who feel entitled believe there is no fight as they are right and everyone else is wrong. Their behavior, words, and treatment of others are justified because nobody can or should come against them. You would think that it would cause there not to be any competition, right? What's good for me is good for me, and what's good for you is good for you. Everyone wins. That is not always the case.

When everyone is out for themselves, there can be a sense of *entitlement.*

They believe they have a right to something. Nobody can challenge them. They will do whatever it takes to protect and procure what they

---

[45]    James 4.1-3, NIV

believe is rightfully theirs. Therein lies the spirit of competition. There may be an appearance, although a false one, that they care about the rights of others. Yet, for someone who has a spirit of entitlement, the only *rights* they care about are their own. When someone believes they are *entitled* to something, they will often do whatever they can to obtain it. It doesn't matter if they hurt someone else in the process.

I believe that part of the problem is that we are all wounded, and we do all we can to protect ourselves, even if it means winning at all costs. Our wounded spirit, or our brokenness, can cause us to either relinquish our true rights or cause us to fight viciously for what we are afraid of losing. When it comes to conflict, we need to realize that everyone has their own war stories, battles, struggles, and scars. Everyone is wounded. Unfortunately, most people tend to operate out of their woundedness without realizing it. They inflict pain on other people, usually those who care the most about them or those they love the most. They haven't figured out how to navigate their pain, and intentionally or not, they handle it by inflicting pain on others. They may not even intend to hurt someone. However, as my daughter taught me recently, everything said and done impacts other people, one way or another.

I forget where I read it, but someone once wrote about stones being thrown into a body of water. If you didn't see someone throw the stone into the water, you would still know that it happened by the ripples in the water. Those ripples spread out across the water and often make it to the other side. What we do and what we say can create ripple effects that reach people on distant shores or future generations, whether for good or bad. *I am very much aware of what has been called* generational sins, *or* sins of the father. The negative impact of what we say or do can have huge consequences as it hits the shores of someone else's life—in their heart, soul, mind, and body.

STRAINING AT THE OARS

I believe that right behind the waves of competition come the waves of conflict. A spirit of competition that comes from a place of self-centeredness, even from a sense of entitlement, brings about great internal and external conflict. And right behind the wave of conflict comes the wave of confrontation. *Have you picked up on my alliteration?* I do enjoy alliteration, where the points being made all begin with the same letter. In this chapter, I address three C's: *Conflict, Competition, and Confrontation.* As much as we are up for a good challenge and unknowingly perhaps thrive on competition, most people do not enjoy conflict for the simple reason that eventually, it leads to a *confrontation.*

I do not desire conflict, nor do I seek it. At the same time, I know conflict can be good. I'm sure we all want to do whatever we can to avoid conflict and adversity. Or we want to actually overcome conflict and work through adversity. Yet, the ways we deal with conflict don't always go well. When conflict arises, we may avoid confrontation because of how bad it went when we confronted someone in the past. But, even more importantly, most people probably avoid confrontation due to their lack of knowing how to confront someone in a healthy manner.

Over the past several years, as I have been overseeing staff and developing leaders, I have discovered that most people do not know how to be assertive. Most people tend to be aggressive, passive, or passively aggressive. There is great confusion over what it means to be assertive. To many people, being assertive means getting what you want, which is usually done aggressively. Therefore, most people, not wanting to be self-centered, or coming across as entitled for fear of seeming to be competitive, do not know how to be assertive. They instead operate out of passive-aggressiveness, unaware that they are operating from a self-centered nature. Or they do nothing about the situation and become passive. This only causes more personal wounds, which causes the internal struggle about the need to fight for their perceived rights, which feeds the competitive spirit. The cycle is never-ending.

It all boils down to another *c*-word, *communication*. I have been around long enough to realize that communication truly is the key to successful relationships. I have also learned that it is hard to develop healthy communication skills. When conflict arises, the natural innate reaction is to respond aggressively, passively, or passive-aggressively. We can't help ourselves probably because we have never seen healthy communication modeled in any relationship.

The secret to surviving the waves of *conflict* is found in learning how to be assertive, which requires having healthy *communication* skills. Being assertive means being able to communicate your needs to another person. It's not about demanding your needs. It's not about claiming your rights or throwing your weight around. It's recognizing that we all have needs. If we cannot communicate those needs, others will not be able to meet those needs adequately. As you can probably guess, our unspoken needs that go unmet create within us a resentful spirit, a root of bitterness. Eventually, we wound others with our aggressive response, make ourselves feel better with our passive-aggressive behavior, or retreat into passivity.

It will take another book to discuss how to increase your ability to be assertive. It may be enough to determine how you react to the waves of *conflict* or even how to handle the waves of *competition* or *confrontation*. Are there people in your life who bring out the worst in you? Do you find yourself always competing with them? Are there people who tend to constantly be against you, creating conflict and making it hard for you to even be around them? What keeps you from being able to confront the situation or the person? Do you lack the skills to have difficult conversations? Do you avoid conflict? When you do encounter conflict, how do you typically handle it? Do you fly off the handle? Do you tip into an aggressive nature?

Do you speak without thinking? A good motto to follow is to *measure twice and cut once*. It's a motto that any woodworker says will save them a lot of painful mistakes. Before they cut a piece of wood, they check their measurement one more time. They know that if you cut off the wrong amount, you can't put the wood back on if it's too short. When it comes to communication, whether it's a spoken word, a text, or an email, as another saying goes, *you can't put the toothpaste back in the tube*. Once you say what you say, you can't take back the words or undo the send button. The damage has been done.

No wonder James tells us to be quick to listen and slow to speak—that will help us be slow to become angry.[46] There is nothing wrong with being angry, but don't allow your anger to lash out at others and wound them. When conflict arises, maybe you avoid it through a passive-aggressive nature. You don't address the conflict directly. You skirt the issue, make comments that you hope the other person will pick up on, and behave in a way that will make them wonder if they have done something wrong. You're hoping then they will bring up the matter and allow you to address what is going on. There is no need for you to do the confronting—phew. Being passively aggressive is a tactic in which you try to manipulate the other person or even hurt them by inflicting subtle pain through seemingly gentle comments or behavior. It could be that when conflict arises, you simply avoid it. Are you the passive kind? Do you put off dealing with the conflict? Avoid confrontation? Or defriend them from your social networks? Turn your cart around at the supermarket when you see them in the aisle you were about to go down? Kyle Idleman, in his book *AHA*, talks about putting off the necessary work we need to do to make changes in our

---

[46]    James 1.19, NIV

life—*passivity, procrastination,* and *defeatism.* They can be the same reasons we put off dealing with conflict or confrontation.

With *passivity,* there is the tendency to believe that everything will work out. It could be that you just continue to live as though nothing is wrong. That is exhausting—it is a definite time of *straining at the oars.* With *procrastination,* there is a desire to put off something that may be harmful. In the meantime, we are only hurting ourselves and others. With *defeatism,* we buy into the lie that nothing will ever change, no matter what we do. That can lead to further issues and problems down the road.

You may want to take some time before reading on. Are there any relationships that you are struggling with? Process whether it's due to a spirit of competition, a recent conflict, or because you do not want to confront the person. If there is an unresolved conflict or a confrontation that needs to take place, ask God for the wisdom to know when and how to address whatever is going on. *The References at the back of the book provide some good tools for having these tough conversations.*

# Part Two
## Releasing and Receiving

(*Navigating the Storms of Destruction*)

"Shortly before dawn He (Jesus) went out to them, walking on the lake."[47]

T he disciples are *in the middle of the lake*. It is just before dawn, a new day is about to begin, and now, the light of the world is coming to them. There is about to be another change in the weather. It is time for the disciples to release the oars as Jesus comes to them.

I want to encourage you to trust that no matter what you are going through, Jesus is coming. He is already here. It's time to let him into the boat. It's time to begin *releasing* the oars and *receiving* what Jesus wants to give you as you pay attention to what God is saying and doing. God is always speaking to us. God is always at work. We just need to tune into his voice and look for where he is at work. In order to do that we need to set down the oars and release them. There will come a time to pick them back up, but you won't have to strain to move in God's direction. It's not easy to let go of the oars. They become a comfort. They become our security blanket. It's what we are used to. We are afraid we won't know what to do

---

47    Mark 6.48, NIV

if we are not *straining at the oars*. Plus, while we have the oars in our hands, it's a way for us to remain in control of our lives, or so we think. If we want to receive what God has for us going forward, we need to release the oars as we truly *let go and let God* do what he has in store for us.

As you pay attention to God's voice and notice what he is doing, he will undoubtedly ask you to release some of those areas of your life you've been trying to hold onto. Those things are perhaps keeping you from reaching the other shore. So go ahead, loosen your grips, and allow the Holy Spirit to gently help you set down your oars. It's better than having the Holy Spirit rip them out of your hands.

So, here we go. It is almost dawn. A new day is coming. God wants us to draw near to him as he draws near to us, even though there is no spatial distance. He wants us to stop *straining at the oars*, resisting what he is trying to tell us or show us, and instead to be receptive to what he is doing, even in the midst of the storms. It's amazing what can happen when we just set down the oars. It's responding to the invitation of Jesus, "Come to me, all who labor and are heavy laden, and I will give you rest."[48]

I love how Eugene Peterson translates Jesus' words in The Message,

> "Are you tired? Worn out? Burned out on religion?
>
> *Straining at the oars?* (My addition)
>
> Come to me. Get away with me and you'll recover your life. I'll show you how to take a real rest. Walk with me and work with me—watch how I do it. Learn the unforced rhythms of grace. I won't lay anything heavy or ill-fitting

---

[48]    Matthew 11.28, ESV

on you. Keep company with me and you'll learn to live freely and lightly."[49]

As we draw near to God and fix our eyes on Jesus, we become receptive to the blowing winds of the Holy Spirit. I believe that the apparent *storms of destruction* will *pass* as the winds begin to die down and the violent waves begin to calm, not as the circumstances begin to change, but as we begin to trust and believe that God is with us, that He is in control, and that He is doing a new thing. That is what the disciples experienced as Jesus appeared on the scene.

The Psalmist knew this to be true in life's turbulent times. He proclaims to God, "You rule over the surging sea; when its waves mount up, you still them."[50]

As Jesus came to the disciples, *walking on the lake*, the disciples thought he was a ghost. They were terrified. They could have easily started rowing fast and hard, putting distance between themselves and this *ghost*. Instead, when they heard Jesus' voice saying, "Take heart; it is I. Do not be afraid," I believe they slowly began to set down their oars. "Then he (Jesus) climbed into the boat with them, and the wind died down,"[51] and "the wind ceased."[52]

Whatever you are going through, whatever it is that is causing you to grow weary, tired, and exhausted from the *straining at the oars* you continue to cling to, it is time. It is time to release the grip and respond to the blowing winds of the Holy Spirit. Allow Jesus to come into your life and recognize that he has been with you all along. In his classic writing, *The Pursuit*

[49]  Matthew 11.28-30, MSG
[50]  Psalm 89.9, NIV
[51]  Mark 6.51, NIV
[52]  Mark 6.51, ESV

*of God*, AW Tozer reminds us of the *divine immanence* of God. Tozer writes, "Wherever we are, God is here."

Jesus had to come to the disciples on the lake. There was a physical distance between the disciples and Jesus. With the death and resurrection of Christ and by the outpouring of the Holy Spirit, we can now recognize, if we choose to, that God is with us—always. He is in the boat, storms, desert, and wilderness because the eyes of our hearts have been opened to his presence. We can proclaim amid our storms that *God is here*.

Unfortunately, we don't necessarily pay attention to God's presence or what he does when troubles come. Instead, we grip the oars tighter and attempt rowing as fast and hard as possible. In so doing, there becomes an apparent distance between God and us.

That's what the Israelites did while in the wilderness, whining and complaining to Moses. They blamed him for their predicament, eventually taking matters into their own hands and creating what they thought would be a better solution: an idol. We need to heed the warning, "Today, if you hear His voice, do not harden your hearts, as at Meribah, as on the day at Massah in the wilderness."[53]

Note what Mark says about the disciples and their hardened hearts, "And they were utterly astounded, for they did not understand about the loaves, but their hearts were hardened."[54] The disciples' *hearts were hardened* because they didn't understand what Jesus had done just before this episode in the boat. How were they then going to understand what Jesus was doing now?

Even as we begin to release the oars, it will take some time for our hearts to become soft, pliable, and attentive to what God is doing. We may lack trust. We may be gripped by fear. Our pride may still need some breaking.

---

[53]   Psalm 95.7b-8, ESV
[54]   Mark 6.51b-52, ESV

Perhaps it's time for you to stop—right now—take a pause, be still, and wait for God to begin putting the wind back into your sails, into your soul. Be still and silent, and allow the Holy Spirit to breathe life into your dry bones. Wherever you have been broken, let God begin to rebuild you. As you begin to set down the oars, as you begin to release everything to God, I believe you will begin receiving what God has always wanted to give you.

For whatever reason, you have not been able to accept all that God has for you. Maybe you don't feel deserving or worthy. Maybe you have been wounded and hurt, and your heart has become hardened. There could be bitterness, jealousy, or envy that has clogged your arteries. It's time to begin allowing God access to those broken, wounded, dry places that have kept you from becoming the person God already sees you as in His eyes. Remember, he saw you and knew who you would become, even before you were conceived. Allow the Holy Spirit to begin restoring, rebuilding and recreating you into the person God created you to be in the first place.

God promises, "I will give you a new heart and put a new spirit in you; I will remove from you your heart of stone and give you a heart of flesh."[55] It is what it means to realize that you are a new creation in Christ as you begin to breathe in the goodness of God, as you begin to feel the Holy Spirit begin to breathe new life into you, releasing streams of living water. You will begin to walk according to who you are in Christ, not who you used to be. You will no longer be identified by your past, by your mistakes and failures, by your hurts and pains, but you will "soar on wings like eagles."[56] No more limping. No more broken bones. You will walk, run and soar into your inheritance as a child of God.

---

[55]    Ezekiel 36.26, NIV
[56]    Isaiah 40.31, NIV

"See what great love the Father has lavished on us, that we should be called children of God! And that is what we are!"[57]

You are a child of God. You are the apple of his eye. You were born to soar. At the same time, keep in mind that you will need to take baby steps to *soar on wings like eagles*. Don't just jump out of the nest. Simply begin putting one foot in front of the other. As you continue to follow him, putting your hope and trust in him, God also promises that you will also *run and not grow weary*. At the same time, it will be just enough to know that you *will walk and not be faint*.

I hope this part of the book will help you take time to be still and silent as you begin to release your oars and that you will begin to receive all that God has for you. This includes the assurance that as you wait on God, as you listen to his voice, and begin to pay attention to what he is doing even in the midst of the storm, you will begin to walk with greater confidence. Then, as you begin to walk, with your eyes on Christ, you will begin to run. Then, as you find strength in God, you will begin to *soar on wings like eagles*. Sometimes, as I know, it will take all you've got to just walk without becoming faint. It's just one step at a time, one moment at a time, one day at a time.

For now, even as you struggle putting one foot in front of the other, it may be time for you to just rest in the Lord, wait upon him, and listen to his voice as he guides you into the future that awaits you. It's time to stop listening to the lies, even the ones you tell yourself, and begin receiving, accepting and believing the Truth. "But when he, the Spirit of truth, comes, he will guide you into all the truth. He will not speak on his own; he will speak only what he hears, and he will tell you what is yet to come."[58] In the following chapters, I want to share what God has for you on the *other*

---

[57]    I John 3.1, NIV
[58]    John 16.13, NIV

*side* of whatever storm you are going through. After the disciples realized that it was Jesus walking towards them on the water, the Gospel of John says, "Then they were willing to take him into the boat, and *immediately* the boat reached the shore where they were heading."[59] I'm not sure what *immediately* means. They got to the shore quicker with Jesus at the helm than they would have if they continued *straining at the oars*. The point is that the disciples got to the other shore, where Jesus wanted them to get in the first place. God has something for us on the *other shore*. Don't forget what God told the Israelites "See, I am doing a new thing! Now it springs up; do you not perceive it? I am making a way in the wilderness and streams in the wasteland."[60] God will make a way through. You just have to release the oars, let Jesus in the boat, and trust that the Holy Spirit will take us to the *other shore*, the new life flowing with new wine. God is going to make all things new. Remember, it's not that your circumstances will necessarily change, but you will have an increased faith, a greater trust and hope in God, as you sense His presence, power, provision and purpose in your circumstances.

As you begin to release the oars, pay more attention to God. Begin to pursue God and seek God. Look for his presence. Look for his provision. Look for his blessings. Listen to him. Delight in him. He will teach you how to pray, not merely for what you want but also for what he wants. He will show you how to live, not for yourself, but for him. He will do that by putting within you the desire to honor him, glorify him, please him, and seek after his will. Perhaps simply pray this prayer of David, "Open my eyes that I may see wonderful things in your law."[61]

---

59    John 6.21, NIV
60    Isaiah 43.19, NIV
61    Psalm 119.18, NIV

I love this, "Take delight in the Lord, and he will give you the desires of your heart."[62]

Hear me right. He will not give you *the desires of your heart* as though he were a genie. He may not always give you what you want, but he will give you what you need. He will put within you what he desires for you and give you the ability to do what he desires for you to do.

You may ask for a slice of rye toast, and instead, God gives you a slice of keto bread because he knows that is what you need. God wants us to ask for the desires, the wants that we have, even if it's a cinnamon roll. However, he wants more than anything for us to trust him to answer according to his perfect will. Jesus said, "Which of you fathers, if your son asks for a fish, will give him a snake instead? Or if he asks for an egg, will give him a scorpion? If you then, though you are evil, know how to give good gifts to your children, how much more will your Father in heaven give the Holy Spirit to those who ask him!"[63]

You may not get that cinnamon roll you were craving, but you will be given the Holy Spirit, who will quench your thirst and satisfy your hunger with more and more of the goodness of God. It is the Holy Spirit who will teach you how to pray for the desires of God. As you seek after God, listen to him, and trust him, he will place within you what he desires for you. You will then have a greater sense of assurance about how you are to pray, even as you pray, "Thy kingdom come, thy will be done, on earth as it is in heaven."[64]

As you continue to experience the storms in your life, God can and will give you what you need to navigate the raging waters. While in the storms or out in the wilderness, you will begin to know God more intimately. You

---

[62]    Psalm 37.4, NIV
[63]    Luke 11.11-13, NIV
[64]    Matthew 6.10, KJV

will learn more about God and who he is while you are still in the midst of the storms. He is the same God you knew before the storms appeared, and as has been said, "the God you knew in the light is the same God in the darkness."

God never changes, even if our circumstances do. God begins to breathe life back into your heart and soul in the storms or the wilderness, even as he renews your mind and restores your body. It's the crucible of suffering, the times in the desert, where we become more and more like Christ. Isaiah refers to it as the *furnace of affliction*, "See, I have refined you, though not as silver; I have tested you in the furnace of affliction."[65]

I hope the following chapters will help you set down your oars, stop the straining, pay attention to Jesus, and let him into the boat, into the storm, and into the darkness. *It's just before dawn.* A new day is about to arrive. Release the oars, let Jesus into the boat, and begin receiving your inheritance as a child of God. As John Bevere writes in his book, *God, Where Are You?*, our character is not so much revealed as it is developed. It's in the *releasing and receiving* that our character is developed, even if it means going through the *furnace of affliction.*

Before I deal with how to release whatever oars you are holding onto with all your strength, let me tell you that it's not necessarily going to be easy. It will require work, a cooperation with the Holy Spirit. It will require another type of *straining*. It's a *straining* forward. It's a good *straining*, though it is not without some hard work, discipline, and tenacity. It's perhaps the definition of Jesus' invitation for you to deny yourself, pick up your cross, and begin to follow him. The next chapter will deal with what it means to *strain forward* to receive all that God has for us.

---

[65]    Isaiah 48.10, NIV

# Chapter 8

# STRAINING FORWARD

**T**he Apostle Paul says, "One thing I do: forgetting what lies behind and *straining* forward to what lies ahead, I press on toward the goal for the prize of the upward call of God in Christ Jesus."[66] It's about pressing on even during the storms of life. Not in our own strength, but in the strength of God and according to who He is calling us to become in Jesus Christ. As we step into what God has prepared for us, we will need to begin to release the oars by letting go of that which has kept us from moving into God's better and preferred future. However, it's not a walk in the park, and there is still work to be done. But it's not something we have to do alone. Remember, God is with us. Jesus is in the boat. He is with us in the storms. Knowing that to be true, we can rest in the joy that ours in Christ Jesus, just as He did for us as He went to the cross. "For the **joy** set before him he endured the cross, scorning its shame, and sat down at the right hand of the throne of God."[67] There may not be complete joy in the midst of the storms, but with our eyes on Jesus, we too can endure what-

---

66    Philippians 3.13-14, ESV
67    Hebrews 12.2, NIV

ever we are going through because of the joy that is awaiting us. That is the truth Paul learned, that he shares with us: "For our light and momentary troubles are achieving for us an eternal glory that far outweighs them all."[68]

The Apostle Paul knew there would be suffering in this world. He also knew that suffering was what had to be endured in order to achieve and receive *the prize of the upward call of God in Christ Jesus.* As we anticipate sharing in the resurrection of Christ, we will also need to expect to share in his suffering. Jesus made it clear, saying, *"whoever wants to be my disciple must deny themselves and take up their cross and follow me."*[69]

Following Jesus Christ means there will be times of *straining forward,* which involves letting go of the past, setting down our oars, trusting, and relying upon him to be our strength and rest. The *straining forward* involves letting go of the oars and letting go of that which keeps us *straining at the oars.* To experience the joy set before us, we are to keep "looking to Jesus, the founder and perfecter of our faith."[70] I like how the Amplified Bible translates, "Looking away from all that will distract us and, focusing our eyes on Jesus, who is the Author and Perfecter of faith [the first incentive for our belief and the One who brings our faith to maturity]…"[71]

We cannot keep looking to Jesus if we are constantly looking back, distracted by all that is in the past. To persevere, endure, to run the race set before us requires letting go of the past, the hurt, the pain, the suffering, and the old. Then we can embrace what God has for us on the other side of what Pete Scazzero calls *the wall—emotionally, healthily,* and *spiritually.* When we let go of what has prevented us from experiencing abundant life

---

[68]   2 Corinthians 4.17, NIV
[69]   Matthew 16.24, NIV
[70]   Hebrews 12.2, ESV
[71]   Hebrews 12.2, AMP

in Jesus Christ, we break into the new and abundant life Jesus came to give us. Yes, there is *straining*, but it's *straining **forward***.

For me, it's like going to the gym. People go to the gym for a variety of reasons. I go to the gym to stay healthy, keep in shape, and perhaps even lose weight. Going to the gym for me, however, is a love-hate relationship. I love it when I'm at the gym. I love how I feel after a good workout. I must admit, I don't love going to the gym; I hate going. That's right. I am not contradicting myself. What I said earlier is *I love it when I'm **at** the gym*. It's the thought of going to the gym that I don't love. I'd much rather stay home and watch television. But once I am at the gym, I do love working out. I love to feel *the burn*. I even love how sore I feel the next day. It's because I know what I am doing is good for me. I know that the hard work, the straining involved in lifting weights, will pay off for me. What I do at the gym makes a difference.

Letting down the oars in our spiritually life-changing journey is not easy. It requires work. Perhaps that's why Paul says that he is *straining forward*. The difference with this kind of *straining* is that we are going *forward*, making greater headway into God's better and preferred future for us.

We often avoid doing the work and don't make any progress forward. We become stuck and settle for how things are, never experiencing what's ahead of us. Other times we simply don't make any forward progress because we have a hard time forgetting the past. We are prevented from going forward because we keep looking to the past. We strain our necks, looking over our shoulders. I will deal with that in the next chapter. For now, it's good enough to know that we are a work in progress.

Paul previously made it clear that he is a work in progress, as you and I are still today. "Not that I have already obtained this or am already perfect, but I press on to make it my own because Christ Jesus has made me his own."[72] Again, I like how the Amplified Bible puts it, "Not that I have already obtained it [this goal of being Christlike] or have already been made perfect, but I actively press on so that I may take hold of that [perfection] for which Christ Jesus took hold of me and made me His own."[73]

Paul is saying that his pressing on is continual, ongoing, and an active decision on his part to keep pressing on. The Greek—*ok, I'm not a Greek scholar, but others have done the work for me*—literally means that Paul is chasing or pursuing Christ. Like Mary, Paul has chosen the *one thing* he is to *do*—pursue Christ with all abandonment. There is to be intentionality in our pursuing God, becoming like Christ, *straining forward* to take hold of all that is ours in Christ. We will never arrive. We will never become perfect. Perhaps that's why Paul says that there is a *straining forward*. It is an ongoing movement. It takes continual work.

Guess what? Although we have to keep working at our faith, knowing that we will never be done, God keeps creating us, perfecting his work. God is not done with us. The promise is this, "He who began a good work in you will bring it to completion at the day of Jesus Christ."[74]

Even in setting down the oars, there is work that will continually be going on. You will not be changed overnight. The Holy Spirit is taking the old and bringing about the new. He begins by taking away what has become a heart of stone over years of our *straining at the oars*, and breathes life into what is becoming a heart of flesh. At the same time, you are called to "work out your own salvation with fear and trembling."[75] *As a side note, it says to work out your own salvation.* You are responsible for yourself. You are not responsible for someone else's salvation, except for perhaps parents

---

72  Philippians 3.12, ESV
73  Philippians 3.12, AMP
74  Philippians 1.6, ESV
75  Philippians 2.12, ESV

who need to train up their children in the way God wants them, to grow uniquely and individually in their personal faith. Yet, even as parents, it's not training them to be what we want them to be, but for them to be who God wants them to be. *Trusting God also brings his good work to completion as they work out their own salvation.*

As God takes me through my life-changing journey, a lot of what has identified me and shaped me up until now must be undone; patterns that have become well-formed, habits that have become second nature, as well as unhealthy attitudes firmly etched in my mind, and negative emotions that run deep throughout my veins. God is still untangling the big knot that has choked the life out of me, so that I can experience the abundant life of Christ more fully and confidently.

Someone once described what was going on inside of me like a golf ball. Did you ever take a golf ball with a crack and peel away the outer material? What you discover are tightly wound rubber bands. I was wound up like those rubber bands. If you start unraveling the rubber bands, eventually, you get to the inner core, a rubber ball that is now set free to bounce all over the place. It's like the joy of Christ that leaps from our hearts once the Holy Spirit begins unraveling all that has restricted us from becoming who God is calling us to become.

Unfortunately, we have a hard time *straining forward* due to the intense desire not only to keep looking to the past, but holding tightly onto the past. Even when something has come to an end, we tend to have difficulty letting go. The past is all we have ever known, and sometimes, even though it may have been painful, it's what is familiar, and in some ways, comfortable. In order to move forward, there are times when we must allow there to be an ending to something in the past. Yet, it takes time to allow something to end or bring it to an end on our initiative. Henry Cloud's book *Necessary Endings* deals with the struggle we all have with endings *necessary* for us to move forward, gain healing, and grow and mature. This is especially true when the *ending* is unexpected or thrust upon us—the death of a loved one, divorce, unemployment, and so on.

Unfortunately, many of us struggle with deciding to end what we know needs to end, including a toxic relationship. It is often easier to keep things the way they are and stay with what we have become accustomed to—what is familiar and comfortable—even if it is not the life we were created to enjoy.

In his book *Necessary Endings*, Cloud says that we do not make certain necessary endings because:

1. we hang on too long when we should end something now
2. we do not know if an ending is necessary or if *it* or *he* is fixable
3. we are afraid of the unknown
4. we fear confrontation
5. we are afraid of hurting someone
6. we are afraid of letting go and the sadness associated with an ending
7. we do not possess the skills to execute the ending
8. we do not even know the right words to use
9. we have had too many and too painful endings in our personal history, so we avoid another one
10. when they are forced upon us, we do not know how to process them, and we sink or flounder
11. we do not learn from them, so we repeat the same mistakes repeatedly.

Cloud says, "Somewhere along the line, we have not been equipped with the discernment, courage, and skills needed to initiate, follow through, and complete the necessary endings. We are not prepared to go where we need to go. So we do not clearly see the need to end something, or we maintain a false hope, or we just are not able to do it. As a result, we stay stuck in what should now be in our past."

And it is not only the endings that we must proactively execute that are problematic. There are also the endings that are forced upon us, endings we do not choose, but ones that we also cannot navigate through very well. These endings can include divorce, being fired or laid off, the death of a loved one, the disintegration of a friendship, chronic illness, and so many others. We do not choose these endings—they are thrust upon us by people we have trusted or sometimes by horrible events in life. If we are not prepared or have never experienced these kinds of losses before, these unexpected endings can render us broken, depressed, and floundering, sometimes for years.

Take time to consider what *necessary ending* needs to happen for you to move forward. Perhaps it's time to end an abusive relationship, or begin putting boundaries in place. It could be leaving a job that has a hostile work environment. Look at the list above and consider what might be preventing you from making that decision. Then, whatever reason you might have for not making a *necessary ending*, take it to the Lord, release it to him, and receive what you need to take the next step, whatever that might be. The following chapters just might help you in that process.

# Chapter 9

# RELEASING DARKNESS AND RECEIVING LIGHT

or you were once darkness, but now you are light in the Lord."[76] As
you begin to release the oars in your life, I do believe that you will
begin to move from a time of darkness into light. It's when you will
begin to feel the winds blow into your sails. To fully capture the power of
the wind to begin moving in the direction God wants you to go, you have
to raise the sails.

If the wind is going to move the boat forward, the sails need to be ready
to receive the slightest gust of wind. The sails are no good, all folded up
neatly on the boat. Once again, I know, who am I to write about another
boat or sailing directive? I am not a seaman or a sailor. I don't even know
the difference between port and starboard or what it means to *batten down
the hatches*. A sailboat relies on the wind blowing into the sails, and I have
no idea how to raise or adjust them to move in the direction I want the
boat to go. So, give me some license here as I use another sailing analogy.

---

[76]     Ephesians 5.8, NIV

One way to lean into what God is doing is to draw near to him as you begin to release the oars. Take the time to allow the wind of the Holy Spirit to begin to move you in the direction God wants us to go. It's allowing the Holy Spirit access to breathe into your heart, soul, mind, and body. I have spent times in the morning *breathing in* and *breathing out*. I recently heard the phrase *smell the flowers, blow out the candles*. It's about allowing a focus on the presence of the Holy Spirit as you fill your lungs with air and receive the goodness of God as he expands your faith and massages your heart. It's inviting the Holy Spirit to keep our hearts soft, compliant, and ready for God to work and move in our lives. Too much of what we encounter in the world, even in the church, can harden our hearts and make us insensitive to the movement of God, making it so that we cannot have empathy and compassion for others, let alone the ability to love God with our heart, soul, mind, and body. The practice of breathing in and out is like the breath of the Holy Spirit, giving cleansing and healing, creating within us a new heart. If allowed, the Holy Spirit can remove whatever might be unhealthy or impure from within our heart, soul, mind, and body as we breathe out in order to breath in the goodness of God.

When I imagine raising the sails, it's as though I am allowing God to expand my faith and to increase my trust so that I can receive His goodness to an ever-increasing measure. As the crew on a boat raises the sails, they are positioning themselves to pick up the slightest movement of the wind in order to begin making movement. When you *raise the sails* it's like positioning yourself to allow the Holy Spirit and the breath of God to blow into your heart and soul so that you can begin to experience the nearness of God. Imagine it being the exact thing God did as he breathed life into Adam and Eve. It's the life of God restoring, refreshing, rebuilding, and redeeming us. When the winds begin to blow, the nudging of God could be causing us to raise the sails in order to join in what he is doing.

As we take time to breathe in the goodness of God, by receiving the Truth of the Holy Spirit, God begins to work within us. "For it is God who works in you, both to will and to work for his good pleasure."[77]

Hear me out. Do not start raising the sails too quickly. Remember the woodworker motto *measure twice*, maybe three or four times, *cut once*. Wait upon the Lord and wait again. Then, as you wait, watch for his movement. As Moses once said, "If your presence will not go with me, do not bring us up from here."[78] Too often, we want to go ahead of God and start taking matters into our own hands. It's as though we appreciate all God has done to this point, and then we say, *I got it from here*. We want to take the reins. It's as if God has passed off the baton to us, and now it's up to us to keep moving forward. I recently saw a sign that said *if God is your co-pilot, switch seats*.

So, before you go off on your own, wanting to begin blazing a trail, it could be that God has more for you to receive before you begin *raising the sails*. Maybe you need to take time to be still and quiet, listen, wait, and watch for God's presence to go ahead of you. Breathe in—breathe out.

You might have the temptation to start picking up your oars again, convinced that you must be doing something. It's our human nature to want to go back to the familiar, the similar, the comfortable, and even allow ourselves to believe that we must do something once again. We can't just sit and be still when there's so much work to be done, even good work or spiritual work, to please God and others. It's tempting to pick the oars up. Don't do it. Resist it. Even before you begin to raise the sails, just take time to stop and be still and silent. God invites you to "Be still and know that I am God."[79]

---

[77]   Philippians 2.13, ESV
[78]   Exodus 33.15, ESV
[79]   Psalm 46.10, NIV

Raising the sails could be seen as lifting your eyes to God. It's about looking to God, rather than constantly focusing on your circumstances. Worship the Lord and *gaze upon his beauty.*[80] In so doing, God will lift you *high upon a rock.*[81] God will lift you up on wings like eagles, He will allow you to soar above the storms, above your circumstances, high above the raging seas. He will give you His perspective. He will give you an eternal perspective. Don't begin trying to move in the darkness. Wait for the Light of Christ to begin to show you the way. Even as you may start making plans, let God guide your steps. Allow the Word of God to be the lamp unto your feet.

Sometimes in life, we need to stop and be still, even silent. Our lives are so busy, full of activity and noise, that creating time to do absolutely nothing can be uncomfortable and unfamiliar. Well, not absolutely nothing. We all need periods of silence, isolation, stillness, and setting aside our chores and duties, even our obligations. To be filled up, to hear the voice of God, to begin looking for ways that we might *run with endurance the race that is set before us.* Whatever your race is right now, there are some things to consider. It is a marathon, not a sprint. Your race is not my race, nor is my race your race. We cannot endure the race, let alone finish the race well, if we don't take time to be still, get refreshment, to wait upon the Lord.

One of my other favorite movies is called *Wind*. It stars Matthew Modine as a competitive yacht racer and includes many adventurous moments. There are times when waves are breaking over the boat, and the winds are almost toppling over the yachts. Then there is my favorite moment.

During one of the races, the yachts are at a standstill. There is no wind, no movement. All they could do was lower their sails and wait, then wait some more. It probably felt like an eternity of waiting. You can was not

---

[80]    Psalm 27.4, ESV
[81]    Psalm 27.5, ESV

what they signed up for. They were beginning to feel defeated and discouraged. There are periods of stillness in life when nothing see the anxieties rising in the crew members on the boats. There is frustration and boredom. This was a big race. Waiting in still water seems to be going on, when there may not be a sense of purpose or progress. It can come at any moment; even when you are going full speed ahead, everything can come to a standstill. It is something everyone needs to be prepared for—and dare I say even experience—and a time when the brakes seem to be slammed, and your life comes to a screeching halt.

The pandemic made it clear that I needed stillness—I needed to put some things on pause, be still, and pay attention to what was going on in my heart, soul, mind, and body. That is not something that comes easily to me. Even in times of quiet and stillness, when I can focus on my heart, soul, mind, and body, I can still have this sense that there is something I could be doing, more that I should be doing. After all, you and I were created for a purpose, "For we are his workmanship, created in Christ Jesus **for good works**, which God prepared beforehand, that we should walk in them."[82] We were created *for good works*. We were created to be like Christ. We were created to do the will of God. We were created to do what he designed us to do. The keyword is *walk*. We were created to *walk*—with Jesus, like Jesus, for Jesus. There is to be an ongoing movement forward. Doing *good works* will keep us moving forward. We were made to *soar*, but it begins by walking, putting one foot in front of another. Unfortunately, sometimes just walking seems like I am going nowhere. It's like being on a treadmill. I am working hard—walking fast—but not getting anywhere.

Unless I take time to be still, to pause what I am doing, I will just keep wandering without any purpose. When I turn off the treadmill, get off the

---

[82]    Ephesians 2.10, ESV

track, and stop running this race that is going nowhere, I can hear God's still small voice whispering into my soul, "This is the way, walk in it."[83]

Again, Jesus says, "Come to me, all you who are weary and burdened, and I will give you rest." He then says, "Take my yoke upon you and learn from me, for I am gentle and humble in heart, and you will find rest for your souls. For my yoke is easy and my burden is light."[84] In other words, Jesus wants to carry your burdens so that you can rest in his strength. He is inviting you to set down the oars. Allow him to take off the yoke you are carrying, perhaps the burdens of life and even the laws of Christianity or the burden of being *religious*. He invites you to receive his grace and mercy as you commit to following him. The grace of God can and will keep your heart from becoming hardened, preventing you from taking matters into your own hands and from resisting his movement, voice, and presence.

His yoke is easy, and his burden is light. Jesus took on the weight of our sins upon Himself, so that we can walk in the light of God's glory and grace. However, at the same time, following Jesus, even as he carries our burdens, is not a walk in the park. Jesus said that if we want to follow him and learn from him, we have to deny ourselves, our abilities, and our pride as we pick up the costly price of following him. Yes, it will come with a price. There will be struggles and difficulties, although the other way is worse: trying to do it on our own. As Jesus went to the disciples in the middle of the storm, so He comes to us in our storm, in our darkness, and into the dark night of our soul. He invites us to *come to him*.

As Jesus comes to you, He is inviting you to draw near him, trust in him, and rest in him. He wants you put down your oars, your burdens, and begin to take on his yoke—he has already taken our yoke and the burden

---

[83]    Isaiah 30.21, ESV
[84]    Matthew 11.28-30, NIV

of our sins upon himself, and as He died on the cross He declared, "It is finished."[85]

It is not easy for us, even as Christians, to trust that *it is finished*. We continue to *work out our salvation* as though Jesus didn't *finish* the work on the cross. He may have forgiven us—but we convince ourselves that we need to continue *straining at the oars* of our faith in order to keep God loving us. To put down our oars means to trust in the *finished* work of Christ on the cross. Then it requires us to rely upon the transforming power of the Holy Spirit as we cooperate with what God wants us to do, not in order to secure our salvation, but so that we might become who God already knows we are in Christ. It's not about what we do, but what Christ has already done. It's not about what we continue to do, but what the Holy Spirit does within us. It can be hard to let go of the control we falsely believe we have over our own salvation.

The truth is that Jesus did the work. He paid the price for our sins, *it is finished*, and we no longer have to earn God's forgiveness or salvation. However, as we are being transformed, the process of sanctification by the Holy Spirit continues. Remember, you and I are not finished products. Yet, even when it comes to our sanctification, our default response, our knee-jerk reaction, and our old way of living is to pick up the oars again and begin operating by the flesh and not by the Spirit. Working out our salvation is a good thing.

James said it well, "For as the body apart from the spirit is dead, so also faith apart from works is dead."[86] Faith without actions is dead. However, our faith becomes more religious, *straining at the oars* if it is merely a function of the flesh and not in cooperation with the Holy Spirit. When we operate in the flesh, there are a couple of things going on. We are telling

---

[85]   John 19.30, NIV
[86]   James 2.26, ESV

God, *thanks, but I've got it from here*, indicating that we don't need his help anymore. The truth is that we will always need God's help to do the work we are called to do by faith. Does God need our help? Does God need us to take over? No. What God desires is for us to cooperate with him. He wants us to be "co-workers with Christ."[87] He needs our help to bring about his complete work in us. Yes, we need to cooperate with God. Yes, we are responsible for living according to our part of the covenant of grace. However, only God will ultimately bring about the necessary and final change.

The Apostle Paul knew this firsthand: "I planted, Apollos watered, but God gave the growth."[88] All the planting we do, all the watering that takes place, will only produce fruit in our lives by the work of God. We cannot make fruit grow or eliminate the bad fruit and replace it with good fruit. The fruit produced in our lives results from the Holy Spirit working within us, changing, transforming, renewing us, getting rid of the old, and giving us the new.

We have to yield to the work of God. We have to be honest with God and ourselves. We have to let him do the pruning. We cannot try to bring about the results on our own or even manipulate things to go the way we want them to. Or else we will find ourselves trapped and stuck, unable to produce the fruit that Jesus says will last, the eternal fruit. We will try taking down some of the bad fruit and using Velcro to produce new fruit. It will not last. Only God can purge us of the bad fruit. Only through the Holy Spirit can God begin to give us what is necessary to produce the good fruit, the lasting fruit, the eternal fruit. God wants us to produce fruit that

---

87    I Corinthians 3.9, NIV
88    I Corinthians 3.6, ESV

will not get spoiled but bring about a greater harvest. As Jesus said, "A good tree cannot bear bad fruit, and a bad tree cannot bear good fruit."[89]

It's not about the fruit at all. It's about having a healthy tree. And to have a healthy tree goes back to what Jesus says, "Already you are clean because of the word that I have spoken to you. Abide in me, and I in you. As the branch cannot bear fruit by itself, unless it abides in the vine, neither can you, unless you abide in me. I am the vine; you are the branches. Whoever abides in me and I in him, he it is that bears much fruit, for apart from me you can do nothing. If anyone does not abide in me he is thrown away like a branch and withers; and the branches are gathered, thrown into the fire, and burned. If you abide in me, and my words abide in you, ask whatever you wish, and it will be done for you. By this my Father is glorified, that you bear much fruit and so prove to be my disciples."[90]

Notice what Jesus said, *already you are clean because of the word that I have spoken to you*. We have already been forgiven. We have already been cleansed of our sin. What is expected of us is to continue to stay cleansed. Doing that requires us to stay connected to the one who not only forgives us but also gives us life. We do not bring glory to God by doing good things, producing good fruit, or doing what we believe Christians are supposed to do. Those are all by-products of what gives him glory and honor—staying connected to him, the vinedresser, as we abide in Christ.

How do we abide in Christ? By abiding or remaining in His *word* found in Scripture. Even more so, it's allowing the Word of God to speak to you. As you then abide in Christ, as you allow God to reveal to you more about the grace and truth of his love in Christ, the more the Holy Spirit releases streams of living water that produce the fruit that comes from abiding in

---

[89]    Matthew 7.18, NIV

[90]    John 15.3-8, ESV

Christ. Read God's Word, meditate on what you read, take it to heart, and even memorize what you find to be the precious jewels God reveals to you. Journal about what you are reading, what you hear, and experience.

"And he who was seated on the throne said, 'Behold, I am making all things new.' Also he said, '**Write this down**, for these words are trustworthy and true.'"[91] "Then the Lord replied, '**Write down** the revelation and make it plain on tablets so that a herald may run with it.'"[92]

It is also a rich experience and practice to then memorize Scripture. It's not just something children do in Sunday school. Jesus, when tempted by Satan, did not combat him with his brilliant thoughts but with the word of God. We cannot fight the battle by simply using our ingenuity, know-how, or intelligence. Yes, God gives us wisdom, and the Holy Spirit will tell us what to say at the right time. However, we cannot survive or win battles on bread alone, but with every word that comes from God. The Word of God, the Scriptures, the Truth, are used as swords to fight the enemy in our hearts, minds, and souls.

"For this is the covenant that I will make with the house of Israel after those days, declares the Lord: I will put my law within them, and I will write it on their hearts. And I will be their God, and they shall be my people."[93] The Psalmist proclaims, "I have hidden your word in my heart that I might not sin against you."[94]

Spend each day with God by reading, studying, meditating, and even memorizing the Word of God. As you do, you are engaging with Jesus Christ, the living word of God. Develop a plan, use a devotional guide, or start somewhere in the Bible. Begin with the Gospel of John, "In the

---

[91]  Revelation 21.5, ESV
[92]  Habakkuk 2.2, NIV
[93]  Jeremiah 31.33, ESV
[94]  Psalm 119.11, NIV

beginning was the word…" Don't rush through it. Don't try reading it all at once. You may only read two verses and be richly blessed and want to stop, be still, listen to the Holy Spirit, and write down whatever you hear. It is delicious. "How sweet are your words to my taste, sweeter than honey to my mouth!"[95] "Oh, taste and see that the Lord is good! Blessed is the one who takes refuge in him!"[96]

Let me add a very important detail. Moses needed help from Aaron and Hur as he was praying, interceding for Joshua who was on the battle-field.[97] You, too, will need help. You need others praying with you and for you. You need to be in a Christian community, whether the local church, a small group, or a few trusted friends. You do not need to go this alone. You should not go this alone. You cannot fight the battle on your own. Yes, God is always with you, and Jesus is constantly interceding on your behalf. Jesus interceded for you on the cross when he prayed, "Father, forgive them."[98] Yet, He continues to pray on your behalf. While on earth, Jesus spent countless times in prayer, interceding on behalf of others, much like he told Peter, "Simon, Simon, behold, Satan demanded to have you, that he might sift you like wheat, but I have prayed for you that your faith may not fail."[99] By the resurrection and ascension of Jesus, you have been given the Holy Spirit. You now have the presence of God with you daily.

However, there are times you may need Jesus with skin on. You were not meant to live in isolation. You were created to be in community. However, in addition to all of that, you may also need professional help and counseling. I don't know what your wilderness is like or what battles you face

---

95    Psalm 119.103, NIV
96    Psalm 34.8, NIV
97    Exodus 17.12, NIV
98    Luke 23.34, NIV
99    Luke 22.31-32, ESV

even as you read this book. Perhaps there's an addiction or deep depression. There could be past abuses, physical, emotional, or verbal. You may be *straining at the oars* of divorce or even grief. There are great support groups in the Christian and secular communities if you are troubled.

Some people are trained to come alongside you to navigate the often treacherous waters. Some people have experienced what you are going through, even though each person's journey is unique. Don't be afraid to ask for help. God created us all with unique gifts and skills to work together to bring about the greater good of God's people. You are not alone, although you may feel alone. You may experience loneliness, although you are not alone. Yes, God is with you. However, he will surround you with people who can contribute in ways that only they can contribute, with gifts, skills, passions, and experiences that only they can provide.

Think about a boat with an entire crew. You can sail alone, but it's a lot of work. It's exhausting and requires skill and strength. But, when you sail with a crew, everyone on the boat has a place and a job to do. Raising the sails requires everyone to cooperate. Raising the sails by yourself while trying to steer the ship and even battening down the hatches—I looked up the term *batten down the hatches* and will share in the next chapter—can be anyone's undoing.

We also need others to help us stay the course. On our own, we may never fully be confident that we are going in the right direction. For a ship to go from one port to another is not easy to do when you are in the middle of the ocean with no sight of land. Without a compass or navigation device, you could think you are going in the right direction, but with just an inch off course, wind up in another country—or not where you intended. The people you trust and respect in your life, counselors, or fellow followers of Christ, can help you navigate the course. When you are not going in the right direction, they can point it out and even help you stay away from dangerous waters or hazardous obstacles. Ok, I'll say it—they can be your lighthouse. Keep in mind you may not want to hear what they have to say at times. However, the person in the lighthouse can see way more than a boat struggling to make it to the shore. The ship, particularly late at night and battling giant waves, may be unaware of rocks and barriers in their way.

Let me offer a few verses from the Bible that speak to the need for us to have and be the *light of Christ:*

> ➤ "The people walking in darkness have seen a great light; on those living in the land of deep darkness a light has dawned."[100] Notice that the people were walking. However, they were walking in *darkness*. Perhaps they were not walking *in the way of the Lord*. The *light* the Israelites saw was the hope and promise of the Messiah, Jesus Christ, who, while on this earth, said, "I am the light of the world. Whoever follows me will never walk in darkness, but will have the light of life."[101] *I probably don't need to point it out, but did you see the word* walk *again?*

> ➤ "In him was life, and that life was the light of all mankind."[102] Jesus is our *light* and our *lighthouse*. No matter how dark the world around us may become, his light always shines. That is why it is crucial we continue to abide in him. In so doing, you and I not only are given the light of Christ, but we then also become the light of Christ for others.

> ➤ "You are the light of the world."[103] It's not that you are necessarily *the light*. You are a light. *The light,* Jesus Christ, shines in you and from you, driving away the darkness wherever you go. You then

---

[100] Isaiah 9.2, NIV
[101] John 8.12, NIV
[102] John 1.4, NIV
[103] Matthew 5.14, NIV

can live in victory, knowing that *the light* of the world, radiating from within you, drives the darkness away.

➤ "Your word is a lamp for my feet, a light on my path."[104] *Hmm, a lamp for my feet—walking?* Another resource that we have been given is God's holy word. Recall that in John 1, we are told that Jesus was the word made flesh. We walk in his light, abiding in him, as we also abide in the written word of God.

We have the light of Christ to shine in us and through us. We have the Holy Bible as a light to guide us through times of darkness. And as I mentioned earlier, one of the ways God enlightens us is through the gift of the Holy Spirit. "What we have received is not the spirit of the world, but the Spirit who is from God, so that we may understand what God has freely given us."[105] Not only does the Holy Spirit illuminate the way for us by interpreting the word of God, but he also illuminates the way for us by revealing to us the will of God. The Holy Spirit enlightens us as he redeems us and restores us by renewing our minds. It is then that we are empowered to walk according to God's good and acceptable and perfect will.[106]

Jesus said, "Whoever walks in the dark does not know where they are going."[107] Jesus also said, "Whoever follows me will never walk in darkness, but will have the light of life."[108] *Yep, there is the word* walk *again.* "For you have delivered me from death and my feet from stumbling, that I may walk before God in the light of life."[109] *I know you saw it*—walk. The Holy Spirit within us ultimately allows us to walk in the light of Christ.

---

[104] Psalm 119.105, NIV
[105] I Corinthians 2.12, NIV
[106] Romans 12.2, ESV
[107] John 12.35, NIV
[108] John 8.12, NIV
[109] Psalm 56.13, NIV

Read the following verses about *light* and meditate on them. Ask God to continue to expose any darkness you may still be walking in or drive away any darkness enveloping you.

"You, Lord, are my lamp; the Lord turns my darkness into light."[110]

"Blessed are those who have learned to acclaim you, who walk in the light of your presence, Lord."[111] I hate to be redundant, but there it is again, *walk*.

"The eye is the lamp of the body. If your eyes are healthy, your whole body will be full of light. But if your eyes are unhealthy, your whole body will be full of darkness. If then the light within you is darkness, how great is that darkness!"[112]

"This is the message we have heard from him and declare to you: God is light; in him there is no darkness at all."[113]

"He will bring to light what is hidden in darkness and will expose the motives of the heart."[114]

"For at one time you were darkness, but now you are light in the Lord. Walk as children of light."[115] *Ah ha—walk! I*

---

[110]    2 Samuel 22.29, NIV
[111]    Psalm 89.15, NIV
[112]    Matthew 6.22-23, NIV
[113]    I John 1.5, NIV
[114]    I Corinthians 4.5, NIV
[115]    Ephesians 5.8, NIV

*may need to write another book just on the concept of walking in the Bible.*

"And this is the judgment: the light has come into the world, and people loved the darkness rather than the light because their works were evil."[116]

"But you are a chosen race, a royal priesthood, a holy nation, a people for his own possession, that you may proclaim the excellencies of him who called you out of darkness into his marvelous light."[117]

"Whoever says he is in the light and hates his brother is still in darkness. Whoever loves his brother abides in the light, and in him there is no cause for stumbling. But whoever hates his brother is in the darkness and walks in the darkness, and does not know where he is going, because the darkness has blinded his eyes."[118]

"But if we walk in the light, as he is in the light, we have fellowship with one another, and the blood of Jesus his Son cleanses us from all sin."[119] *Do I need to point it out? Walk.*

"For God, who said, 'Let light shine out of darkness,' has shone in our hearts to give the light of the knowledge of the glory of God in the face of Jesus Christ."[120]

---

[116]   John 3.19, ESV
[117]   I Peter 2.9, ESV
[118]   I John 2.9-11, ESV
[119]   I John 1.7, ESV
[120]   2 Corinthians 4.6, ESV

"The night is far gone; the day is at hand. So then let us cast off the works of darkness and put on the armor of light."[121]

"In the same way, let your light shine before others, so that they may see your good works and give glory to your Father who is in heaven."[122]

"For it is you who light my lamp; the Lord my God lightens my darkness."[123]

"I have come into the world as light, so that whoever believes in me may not remain in darkness."[124]

---

[121] Romans 13.12, ESV
[122] Matthew 5.16, ESV
[123] Psalm 18.28, ESV
[124] John 12.46, ESV

# Chapter 10

# RELEASING THE PAST AND RECEIVING THE FUTURE

"For I know the plans I have for you," declares the Lord, "plans to prosper you and not to harm you, plans to give you hope and a future."[125] he title of this chapter is *Releasing the Past and Receiving the Future.* In other words, *don't look back.* I could have just as easily called it *Becoming the Person God is Calling You to Become in order to Do What God is Calling You To Do.* We cannot become the person God is calling us to do if we are constantly looking back.

There are times that it will be necessary and beneficial to look at the past. With help, it might be wise for anyone to process significant moments in their life from the past, the good, bad and ugly. There is nothing wrong with looking at the past, as long as the looking back doesn't drag us down and cause us into a spiral filled with regret, guilt and shame. If it's about confessing what we have done in the past that was not God honoring, there's a place for that. If it's about giving God our past in order to be set

---

[125]    Jeremiah 29.11, NIV

free to live in the present as we venture into the future, there's a place for that. Don't do it alone. Have someone, preferably a professional, help give you a healthy perspective of your past. It might be helpful to look at the past and identify where God was with you, at times carrying you, and to then allow that to give you hope for the future. There is nothing wrong with visiting the past once in a while. Just don't live there. There's a lot that can be said about healing the past, but for now, this chapter is about God's preferred future for His children.

As I will share below, Peter, the disciple who seemingly was willing to do anything for Jesus, ultimately failed. It seems he eventually had a problem moving forward. He was looking back and went back to his old familiar ways. Jesus was calling Peter to become the person God was calling him to become. Peter was stuck in the past.

There is nothing wrong with reminiscing, recalling what God has done in the past, processing your life experiences, and acknowledging how your past has impacted who you are today. We can learn from the past and grow and mature to do better in the future. However, we need to keep seeing what God is doing today as he prepares us for tomorrow. Yesterday can impact and influence who we are today. However, let's not allow it to become a stronghold that prevents us from becoming person God is calling us become today and in the future.

As you probably already know, you cannot put new wine into old wineskins. You were created for new wine. You were also created to receive daily bread, God's fresh manna, rather than nibbling on yesterday's stable crumbs. As a pastor, I often said to the congregation on a Sunday morning, "It is my prayer that you are not the same person when you leave as you were when you arrived."

My prayer is that I'm not the same person today as yesterday. I am being transformed and becoming the person God is calling me to become, whether due to or despite my past. No wonder God is constantly transforming and renewing us.

I am not a tech savvy person and do not know how to fix most technological problems. Fortunately, there's Google and YouTube. Unfortunately, I will spend countless hours researching the problem, even into the night. I am like a dog with a bone when it comes to solving problems or fixing issues that I believe have an obvious answer. The same is *not* true if it's something like rewiring the house or fixing our irrigation system.

No matter how much I search or how many hours I research, I am not the guy to fix it even if I discover the answer. After many searches and solved problems, I believe that there is one word for most technological issues—reboot. Turn the power off, give it a minute, turn it back on, or unplug it and plug it back in—problem solved.

Whenever the disciples had a problem, they couldn't Google it. When they were in a bind, I wonder if they went to Peter. I'm sure he would work hard, frantically trying to solve the dilemma. He seemed to be the type who would do whatever he could to fix things or make them right. However, even Peter didn't have all the answers. He certainly did not always have the right answers. Remember, he is the one who supposedly chopped off the ear of a soldier when Jesus was being arrested in the garden. After all his attempts to figure things out, I wonder if he finally said, "Let's ask Jesus. Jesus knows everything." Or did his ego get in the way?

I believe that Peter was an eager and loyal disciple, or so he wanted to be. He wanted to do everything Jesus told him to do—even attempting to walk on water. But as we know, he was just as human as any of us in the end. In his bravado and willingness to do it all, he ran out of steam as Jesus probably felt foolish looking back at some of his mistakes, like cutting off that soldier's ear. So, in the shadows, while Jesus is being led to his death, Peter lingers. Perhaps he is ashamed of his past behaviors, and even now feeling guilty for not being able to rescue Jesus. It could be that now, in Jesus' darkest hour, Peter is afraid for his own life. Given an opportunity to step up and act again, Peter wants nothing to do with what is going on. He denies ever being associated with Jesus—the one he proclaimed he would follow, even if nobody else went with him.

That scene gives me a glimpse into Peter more than any other episode was after the death, burial, and resurrection of Jesus. On the day of the Resurrection, the women who had seen the empty tomb ran to tell Peter and the other disciples that Jesus was alive. It's important to realize that the women were instructed to tell the disciples *and Peter*. Peter was singled out. Would he need more convincing than others that Jesus was alive, and that Peter was to join the other disciples in Galilee, where Jesus would meet them? Peter may not have felt worthy of such an invitation. So, off to Galilee went the disciples *and Peter*.

We don't know how much time had gone by once they arrived at Galilee. However long it was, Peter eventually proclaims to the others, "I am going fishing." Peter was probably saying, "I am going *back* to fishing." *I realize that going fishing is as good as it gets for some. As someone who doesn't fish, that doesn't make any sense.* Remember, Peter was a fisherman when Jesus invited him and Andrew to follow him. So, Peter went back to what he was doing before Christ found him. He goes back to that which was familiar—fishing. It could be, because of his grief, he was looking for something natural, familiar, normal and comfortable. It could be that Peter simply got tired of sitting around doing nothing.

We are probably no different. It was rather refreshing to be told not to do anything during the pandemic. Yet, after several months, particularly as things began to open up, it was easy to find ourselves getting back to what we were doing before the pandemic. There was certainly nothing wrong with that. It's alright to finally be able to do what we used to do.

There is nothing wrong getting back into the routine of our life. However, after whatever pandemics or lifechanging events we go through, could it be that God doesn't always want us to go back to that which is familiar and comfortable?

It could be that Peter went back to fishing because he felt guilty about having denied even knowing Christ. He perhaps believed that he was no longer the rock Jesus would use to build his Church. He had let down Jesus up to the very end. He may as well go back to his career. But, did he also go back to his old life, habits, and routines before He ever met Jesus. Peter was a fisherman when Jesus found him. Jesus though had new plans. He gave Peter a new calling. Peter would be a fisher of people. It could be that Peter went back to fishing because he was looking at his past with shame and regret. He did the one thing he swore he would not do—he denied Jesus publicly. Did he believe Jesus gave up on him and was no longer worthy of being a fisher of people?

Again, our human tendencies and temptations are to base our worth and value on the past rather than on who God calls us to become as new creations in Christ. God created us to keep moving forward. If we keep looking at and perhaps keep being controlled by the past, we may miss what God is doing today as he prepares us for tomorrow.

Just look at our physical bodies. God created us to move forward. Every part of our body, all but one part, is positioned to dictate we should be moving and looking forward. The problem is that we can be walking forward while still looking back. That's not natural. That's not how we were created. You can be walking forward while looking backward, but it will be laborious. It could be disastrous because you don't see what's coming.

We were also designed to move forward spiritually. So, rather than surviving on yesterday's stale crumbs, we are to keep growing and maturing, receiving God's daily bread, heavenly manna, fresh and warm right out of the oven. We cannot move into God's preferred future to become who God is calling us to become if we constantly look back to who we used to be. It's especially true if we try to live off of past mountaintop experiences we have encountered or try to recreate what used to fill us up. It's like living in the house you moved into back in the '60s and still living with the same furniture that at one time was shiny and new and even cutting edge. Remember lava lamps? Sometimes we need to get rid of what used to define us or even bring us pleasure. Lava lamps? Really? However, you can't just have a garage sale and call it good. It's not about just getting rid of the past, or the old. Remember, Paul says there isa also a *straining forward*. It's an ongoing process that requires slowly letting go of the past—and that is never easy. We are hoarders. We like to hold onto things. Who knows when we may need that bean bag chair or a lava lamp? I know, lava lamps are becoming vogue again. Really?

Your past could be so painful that it is hard to stop looking in the rearview mirror, being reminded of the damage that marks the highway behind you. With all its pain, your past could be affecting the journey you are on today and preventing you from traveling down the road God is creating before you.

You could be filled with regret, shame, guilt, or even anger for what has happened to you, what you experienced, and how you were treated. The famous theologian Lionel Richie recently said that you'll trip over your future if you keep screaming at the past. (I know—Lionel Richie is not a theologian. But that is good stuff.) If your past keeps you from moving forward, God can heal you, but you may also need someone in the flesh. You may need professional help or pastoral care. Maybe you need to call upon a Christian friend you trust and respect to come alongside you, pray for you, and simply be *Jesus with skin on* for you. I know it can be scary to take that next step. Lionel Richie also said, *life begins at the end of your comfort zone.* Back to Peter and the other disciples going back to fishing in John 21.

As they begin to cast their nets into the water, and after hours of catching nothing, I can imagine the tenacity of Peter. The fight within him was to keep on fishing until he caught something, or until he got some answers, or until his sense of purpose returned. He was not going to quit, even if it took all night. Peter and the rest were out in the boat, casting their net into the water, all night long until the sun came up, and they did not catch one fish. Were they at the end of themselves? Were they again *straining at the oars* and making no progress? *I wonder if they had any vulgar words they uttered under their breath.*

Then, a voice—the voice. A familiar voice. But no, it couldn't be. It says that the disciples didn't know that it was Jesus,[126] but perhaps there was something in them that made them wonder. Whoever it was, he didn't seem to have much empathy for them. They had been fishing all night. Could he not see that they had no fish in their boat? They were exhausted and probably a bit discouraged. Jesus speaks to them from the shore. You can hear him saying, perhaps with a smile, "Good morning. Do you have any fish?" Depending on what translation you use, Jesus addresses the disciples as *young men*, *friends*, *boys*, or *lads*. In the ESV, Jesus addresses them as *children*.[127] In one translation, Jesus says, "You do not have any fish, do you?"[128] I can almost hear the disciples saying quietly, *seriously dude? Are you trying to rub salt into the wound and add insult to injury?* Maybe Peter was ready to roll up his sleeves, jump out of the boat and have a good reckoning of things with this man. After all, not only did this man have the audacity

---

[126] John 21.4, NIV
[127] John 21.5, ESV
[128] John 21.5, HCS

to point out their failure, but he called them *children* or *boys*. Who did he think they were? Was Peter ready to proclaim for Satan to get behind him?

All it says is that when asked the question, or when Jesus pointed out to them that they didn't seem to have any fish, they said, "No." Were their heads hanging down? Were they so exhausted from their evening that they could barely even make a sound? Were they angry at him and themselves because they did indeed have nothing to show for their labor?

Then, whoever he was, this man tells them to try casting their net on the other side. *Try Googling. Try to reboot.* You can almost hear the disciples saying, "Duh," "Who does he think he is?" "Does he not think we've already thought of that?" "Does he think he knows better than us?" "Has he even gone fishing?" "It's a bit arrogant to tell us what to do and then proclaim, *you will find a catch.*"

The disciples had been laboring all night and they did not catch a single fish. Was that all about to change with this man's somewhat prophetic word?

Sometimes, after struggling to move forward and step into the new life that is ours in Christ, we may need to take our foot off the accelerator and try something else. We may need to cast our nets somewhere else. We may need a reboot. To become the person God is calling you to become requires trusting that God is not finished with you yet. You are still in the process of being transformed. To become the person God is calling you to become also means not trying to become the person on your left or right. You have unique spiritual genetic material, your DNA. Consider John the Baptist. Some thought he was Elijah or a prophet, or even Christ himself. He made it clear that he was John, in fact, John the Baptist, and that someone greater than him was coming and was indeed there.

That person was Jesus, who also knew who he was. As John the Baptist baptized Jesus, the confirmation was made from heaven as a voice said,

"You are my son, whom I love; with you I am well pleased."[129] This confirmation came before Jesus had *done* anything. Both John the Baptist and Jesus knew who they were and therefore knew what God had called them to *do*.

To move forward into what God is calling us to become begins with knowing who you are, a child of God, created uniquely by him. By following him, listening to his voice, and waiting upon him, you will become the person God is calling you to become. Day by day, moment by moment, the old is past, and the new keeps coming so that you can do what God is calling you to do. God has created you for a specific purpose. It's not about doing everything or just keeping busy. Doing what God is calling you to do may require doing less than what you've been doing. Doing what God is calling you to do is doing what you are specifically called to do, being confident of who you are. Jesus could do his Father's will, dying on the cross for the world's sins, because he knew who he was and what God had called him to do.

Peter was called to be a fisher of people. However, he returned to catching fish. I believe he forgot who he was becoming when he first chose to follow Christ. So, on the shore of Lake Galilee, while Peter and the others are fishing, the grace of God shows up in Jesus. Without being condescending, Jesus graciously calls out to them, "Children, (or young men or friends), do you have any fish?"[130]

They probably responded with a rejected *no*. Jesus then takes control of the situation and instructs them to cast their nets on the other side of the boat. They had already done that, but Jesus extends grace and says, *try again*. Keep in mind that it was not an easy task to haul up the nets and toss them to the other side of the boat. Even so, perhaps reluctantly, even with a

---

129    Mark 1.11, NIV
130    John 21.5, ESV

rolling of their eyes, the disciples do what this apparent stranger tells them to do. Jesus promised they would *find some* fish.[131]

They actually *found some fish*, but as a result of humbly trusting this stranger, they didn't just catch a few fish, but there were so many fish that it required multiple men to haul them to shore. Grace invites us to *try again*. Grace invites us to *trust again*. Grace invites us to believe that God will *do it again*. He will give us more than we deserve and even more than we can imagine. God "is able to do immeasurably more than all we ask or imagine, according to his power that is at work within us."[132]

Eventually, it says, "That disciple whom Jesus loved, therefore, said to Peter, 'It is the Lord!' As soon as Simon Peter heard him say, 'It is the Lord,' he wrapped his outer garment around him (for he had taken it off) and jumped into the water."[133] What a typical response of Peter—jumping out of the boat. As he jumps into the water, I wonder if he is, in a sense saying that he is done with the past and done with fishing for fish. He is ready to do what Jesus originally called him to do—become a fisher of men.

As Peter and the others eventually make it to shore, Jesus invites them to breakfast. Jesus said to them, "Bring some of the fish that you have just caught."[134] Jesus wants to use what they had worked so hard to get, which was provided to them by God.

In the same way, Jesus invites you to come and have breakfast with him, live in loving union with him, abide with him, and give him everything you have, the good, the bad, and the ugly. Jesus may graciously ask you to trust him as you cast your nets on the other side, or as you drop your nets completely. Begin trusting that you are becoming the person God is calling

---

[131]  John 21.6, ESV
[132]  Ephesians 3.20, NIV
[133]  John 21.7, NIV
[134]  John 21.10, NIV

you to become, receiving the new wine and the fresh daily bread that will never run out or go stale.

Peter was given a second chance or a mulligan, something I am familiar with. I enjoy an occasional round of golf and have played golf as recreation for most of my adult life. I'm proud to say I have improved over time. These days I play in the mid to high eighties and don't play if it gets any hotter than that. My handicap is my driver. The best part of my game is a mulligan. You know what a mulligan is, right? It's the grace of God for golfers like me. Since getting some good clubs, I have taken or been given fewer mulligans. For those of you who are not familiar with the sport of golf, the game of kings, a mulligan is a do-over. If your drive from the tee box goes way out of bounds, or as can be the case of some golfers, does not make it past the next tee box, the rest of your party might offer you a mulligan. You don't count the first stroke. You get to take another swing for free, without penalty.

The Bible is full of mulligans, do-overs, or second chances. Abraham has his wife lie to Pharaoh, saying that she is Abraham's sister, not his wife. God sends a plague, which is truly severe mercy that God uses to spare Abraham. Abraham gets a second chance. He does it again. He lies about Sarah, claiming her to be his sister. Still, God fulfilled His promise to Abraham, that he would become the father of many nations. Then, there's Moses. He kills an Egyptian—yet God still uses him to lead the Israelites out of captivity.

And, what about King David? He not only commits adultery, but he tries to cover it up, and in the end, has the husband of his mistress sent to the frontline where David knows the husband will die. There is also the story of Joseph, whose brothers tried to have him killed. They end up selling him into slavery. It is eventually through Joseph that God gives his brothers a second chance. As his brothers fear for their lives, waiting for

Joseph to give them what they deserve, Joseph proclaims, "Do not fear, for am I in the place of God? As for you, you meant evil against me, but God meant it for good, to bring it about that many people should be kept alive, as they are today. So do not fear; I will provide for you and your little ones."[135] Then, it says Joseph comforted them and spoke kindly to them. Joseph gave his brothers a second chance. A prostitute named Rahab was given a second chance by God and even used by him.[136] She was considered *righteous*.[137]

These are just some of the Old Testament accounts of second chances. There are more in the New Testament. There was Zacchaeus, a deceitful and selfish tax collector, is invited by Jesus to share a meal. He is given a second chance. Jesus provides him salvation.[138] As a result, Zacchaeus repents and gives people back their money with interest. Then, there are the disciples. Some were skeptical, like Andrew and Phillip. James and John, known as the *sons of thunder*, were aggressive and intolerant, and even self-centered. Bartholomew was prejudiced and opinionated. Matthew was a hated tax collector. We don't know much about the disciple called James the younger, his brother Jude, or Simon. And, of course, there's *doubting* Thomas. Let's not forget about Peter. He was a bit of a loose cannon who couldn't keep his mouth shut, a man of contradictions who eventually went against his word and denied Christ three times. As I shared earlier, Jesus gave Peter a second chance. Peter went on to be a great leader in the Church. Unfortunately, one of the disciples, Judas, didn't wait for a second chance. Perhaps he didn't believe he deserved a second chance. Then there is Paul, formerly known as Saul. He was violently persecuting the Christians. He too was

---

135    Genesis 50.21, NIV
136    Joshua 6.25, NIV
137    James 2.25, NIV
138    Luke 19.9, NIV

given a second chance. His transforming encounter with Jesus is told in Acts 9. As Paul was traveling to Damascus, a light shone around him, and *he heard a voice.*[139] It was the voice of Jesus, confronting him, giving him a second chance, transforming him, and sending him on a new path.

It's not about being given a second chance, as it is about what we do with it. We are given an opportunity like Paul to either continue down the path we are on or go in the way of the Lord. We can allow our past to keep us from following Christ. Our past can convince us that we are beyond hope and beyond help. Our past can deceive us into believing our life no longer has meaning or purpose. Or, we can embrace the opportunity given to us, receive the grace and mercy of God, and go down the path that leads to abundant and eternal life. It's a matter of what we do with what is given to us.

Consider the difference between Judas and Peter. Judas didn't wait to be offered a second chance. He could not deal with his past. He could not see a better future. In the end, he took his own life. Peter may have given up and returned to fishing. However, he heard the voice of Jesus calling from the shore and received the grace being extended to him. And then, although a bit reluctant, Peter heeded the invitation to follow Jesus and feed the sheep under his care, even if it led to his own death.[140]

Years ago I learned a little something about the balls that are used in professional baseball. I'm not sure if it still works this way, but at one time, a man came upon some special mud in the swamps in someplace like Florida. This mud was used to scuff up the baseballs before every professional game, allowing pitchers to have a better grip. The balls were rubbed with the mud and then given to the baseball teams to be used for home games. The umpires would grab the balls before a game and rub them a

---

[139]   Acts 9.4, ESV
[140]   John 21.15-22, ESV

little bit to ensure they were of good consistency. A pitcher would do the same before using any ball. If the ball did not feel right, the pitcher would throw it back to the umpire, who would then throw it out of the game. If a ball got smudged by a bat, it would be tossed out of the game. The balls had to be perfect or feel right to the pitcher.

I wonder if sometimes, when we look at our past and consider our life to be smudged, we believe that God throws us out of the game. We may falsely believe that God has no use for us anymore. We strive to be perfect, but we can never attain perfection. Therefore, we give up on ourselves, believing that God has given up on us. I tend to think we do that to ourselves because we do that to others. It is hard to forgive and forget, to live as though something someone did in the past never happened. We may get caught up in seeing people as *smudged*, flawed, and imperfect, then give up on them.

It's time to give God our past, the good, the bad, and the ugly. It's time we stop believing that God will play a video of our entire life when we get to heaven, pointing out all the times we messed up. It's time we trust that God has removed our sins from us, as far as the east is from the west. All our sins were nailed to the cross as Jesus took them all upon himself. He took *all* our sins, past, present, and future. He took them upon himself and buried them in the tomb, where they remain. Let's stop digging them up.

Once again, hear the words of Jesus loud and clear—*it is finished.*[141] Let's stop *straining at the oars* of our past, and instead, let's step into God's preferred future as we continue to receive the grace of God.

---

[141]    John 19.30, NIV

# Chapter 11

# RELEASING THE OLD AND RECEIVING THE NEW

L et me go back to the movie *Wind*. The yachts are in the middle of the ocean, stopped, no wind, sails lowered, a time to just wait. The camera focuses on Matthew Modine, the captain of his crew, peering out into the distance. The camera moves to show us what he sees—ripples on the water. That means the wind is starting to blow again. Matthew quietly gets the attention of his crew. He instructs them to begin raising the sails. They then positioned the sails to begin picking up whatever little bit of wind there was to be caught. Everyone did their part, and before you knew it, they were moving. They were picking up speed. Those little ripples on the water indicated that the waiting was over. Something on the horizon told them they would move once again. They didn't know if it would become what they needed to pick up speed or get to the finish line, but it gave them hope and moved them in the direction they needed to go.

When life is on hold, when there seems to be no movement, no act of God, you just watch and wait. Even while you are waiting, God is at work. Even in times of stillness, God is still moving, God is still at work, and He is making all things new. "See, I am doing a new thing! Now it springs up; do you not perceive it?"[142] The keyword is *now*. Right then and there, in the desert, God was already creating something new at that moment. In the apparent barrenness of life, God is at work creating new life. *Now it springs up.* God's timing is perfect.

At the *right time*, God sent his Son to die for us.[143] While we were considered *enemies of God*[144], alienated and separated from him, Jesus died for us *at the right time.* Into the chaos, darkness, and filth of our world, by the birth of a baby born in Bethlehem, God was doing a *new thing* to set this world on an eternal course. God continues to do something new to us, and in us, through the Holy Spirit, just as He did with the disciples as the resurrected Jesus ascended into heaven. With the gift of the Holy Spirit, God began to breathe new life into the disciples. He didn't wait for them to form a small group, establish committees, or live a few years in their new faith. While they were still grieving, even hiding in fear, the Holy Spirit came and began doing a *new thing*. In the middle of your storms, amid your chaos, while you are waiting for God to move, look for the ripples on the water. God is doing a *new thing*—do you see it? Keep watching. God is doing a *new thing* in your soul, in your relationships, in your attitude, in your perception of things, and even in your faith.

I have lived in regions of the country where there are four seasons. Winter can seem like the longest season. There were times when the sun didn't shine for weeks at a time. There were no leaves on the trees. The snow on the ground made everything appear to be in black and white, but the hope I had was that winter would yield to spring one day. That hope would become real as I watched for little green shoots to appear out of the

---

[142]   Isaiah 43.19, NIV
[143]   Romans 5.6, NIV
[144]   Romans 5.10, NIV

ground. Even as life was beginning to appear, it would occasionally snow again. There was always great rejoicing with every little sprig of green, and every bud on the tree.

Yet, even in the middle of winter there were times of celebrating and rejoicing. There was life in the midst of what seemed dead and barren. In the cold, cold winter, the falling of snow is a beautiful display of God's creation. There is so much awe and wonder when you can hold a few snowflakes in your hand and witness the intricate design of God's creation. It reminds me of my uniqueness, created in the image of God, filled with the beauty and splendor of his majesty. Even in times of winter, God reminds me that I am his *handiwork*. Then, of course, there is Christmas in the darkest of winter—the celebration of Christ coming into our world. From that day on the days get longer, and it's like the light of the Son, the birth of Christ, begins driving away the darkness of winter with God's eternal love bursting into the world. Mary, the mother of Jesus was enraptured with the tiny baby in her arms, pondering what this miraculous birth meant. We too should take the time to ponder the nearness of God in the life of Christ and by the Holy Spirit, as we consider the eternal design of God's plan for humanity.

In the middle of a storm and bleak winter, what ripples do you notice on the water? How can you pay attention to what God is doing? How can you listen to his whisper? What is God calling you to do in preparation to catch the wind in your spirit and your sails? What blessings are you able to identify and celebrate? Maybe write down what you see, sense, hear and praise God from whom all blessings flow.

During the pandemic, a message I heard on the radio used the analogy of a plane in a holding pattern. Life in America and worldwide was placed in a holding pattern when COVID-19 landed on our shores. The message was that we should stay at home, shelter at home, and there should be no gatherings. People were beginning to realize the plans they made for 2020 were not going to happen. That 2020 calendar or daily planner just got shredded. It was as though we were in a holding pattern.

When a plane arrives at its destination, for reasons nobody on the plane will ever know, the pilot is told to stay in the sky, circle, and hang out while things get resolved. It isn't safe to land. So, the pilot puts the plane in a holding pattern. The message I listened to then gave four instructions during a holding pattern. I used those points in my message, tweaking it for our situation and congregation. My message was titled *A Certain Joy in Uncertain Times*. I believe that there is *joy in the journey*, even if the journey seems confusing and uncertain. Here are my lessons from the sermon I heard as I applied them to Habakkuk. I hope they can help you live with certain joy in uncertain times.

First, while seeking certain joy in uncertain times, *don't panic*. The prophet Habakkuk says, "Though the fig tree should not blossom, nor fruit be on the vines, the produce of the olive fail and the fields yield no food, the flock be cut off from the fold and there be no herd in the stalls, yet I will rejoice in the Lord; I will take joy in the God of my salvation."[145] Come what may, Habakkuk proclaims that he will continue to rejoice in God. Habakkuk will not panic in the face of a bleak situation. He will not pick up the oars out of desperation. He is going to trust in the God of his salvation. My favorite words from Habakkuk are, "But the Lord is in his holy temple; let all the earth keep silence before him."[146] *Another call to be silent before God.* Habakkuk can have a certain joy amid a bleak season of life because he knows that God is on the throne, in his holy temple. God is the one who creates the fruit on the vines. He's done it before, and he will do it again.

---

[145]  Habakkuk 3.17-18, ESV
[146]  Habakkuk 2.20, ESV

How is it possible NOT to panic in bleak situations and desperate times? How do I stop letting my imagination get the worst of me, not allowing fear to begin telling me lies, robbing me of the joy of the Lord? Timothy Keller credits his wife with another airplane illustration. When you are on a plane, before taking off, flight assistants always announce that oxygen masks are lowered in an emergency. You are instructed to put your mask on first, before helping someone else put their mask on.

In times of uncertainty, when the enemy is trying to rob you of the joy of the Lord, be sure you take put your oxygen mask on first, taking care of yourself, while being still in the presence of God. Grab the oxygen mask, take a deep breath, and allow the Holy Spirit to fill you with the peace of God, giving the assurance that he has everything in control.

Second, a certain joy in uncertain times comes as you *stay in contact with the control tower. I know; I've gone from boats to planes. Jesus also used many analogies.* As I spend time with my heavenly Father, I receive the peace that passes understanding and all comprehension. I do this by spending time in prayer, reading the Bible, and listening to the truth of the Holy Spirit. I also spend time listening to Christian music of all kinds. After all, Habakkuk chapter 3 is a song. In the end, Habakkuk instructs this prayer, this psalm, to be given to the choirmaster and stringed instruments. This prayer would become a song the Israelites could sing while in exile, reminding them of God's faithfulness, of his promises and covenant. It became a song that would be handed down for generations.

Perhaps there's a song that gives you a sense of peace and comfort or a particular verse in the Bible that you can use to stay focused on things above and not the things below. Perhaps God will give you a new song to sing during these uncertain times.

Third, *stay in your assigned seat* as you seek certain joy in uncertain times. Your life, gifts, situation, experiences, and emotions are yours alone. You are unique. Stay true to who you are in Christ as a child of God. Don't look at the other passengers to see how they respond or what they are doing. Respond to what God is calling you to do in any given circumstance.

Fourth, while in a holding pattern, while waiting for a certain joy to break forth during uncertain times, *be open to an alternative landing site.* You may be going in the direction you thought you were supposed to be going and doing what you thought you were supposed to be doing. You may have made your plans exactly knowing what you wanted out of life. However, you must let God continually guide your steps. God may have a different plan, a better plan. It may not make sense. It may create anxiety and fear within you.

Finding joy in uncertain times is trusting the truth of God: "For those who love God all things work together for good, for those who are called according to his purpose."[147] The wisdom of God is such that he makes the best of times out of the worst of times. He corrects the wrong. He mends what is broken. He makes good what we have made bad. We may think we know where things will be due to COVID-19, but God may have even more in store for us than anything we could ever ask or think possible. Let's not jump out of the plane or bailout during the hard times. Instead, let us press on towards the prize and continue to rejoice in God, our strength, the Lord of our salvation.

Whatever is going on in your life, whatever disruptions you may have recently experienced, are you waiting for your life to change, get better, and go back to *normal?* What if there is no *normal?* You may want life to get back to how it used to be. The reality is that it may never be the same again.

---

[147]    Romans 8.28, ESV

As tempted as you might be, there's no turning back. Then, as you wait on God, keep moving forward, one day at a time, asking God to show what you are supposed to do next. Maybe it's nothing at all. Perhaps, for now, it's just watching and waiting for God to show you the new way.

We need to continue moving forward, walking—perhaps limping as we go—according to God's purpose for our lives, the *good works* that God has prepared for us to do. When life comes to a standstill, God's purpose doesn't stop. We are God's *handiwork, created in Christ Jesus to do good works.*[148] We are God's *masterpiece.*[149] God is the *potter*, and we are the *clay. We are all the work of his hand.*[150] God is the artist, and we are the canvas. God is our master builder, and we are always a work in progress. We may be flawed and scarred, smudged by our choices and circumstances. However, in the end, God uses everything for his ultimate purpose and plan in our lives. Nothing is wasted by God.

Whatever you are going through right now, God is still creating you as his *work*. Like a sculptor looking at a piece of granite, God saw you before creation, he knew the plans he had for you from the beginning, and he knew who you would become. Along the way, he is still crafting you into his image. It may not look like the image you had in mind, but God is the master builder, and we are his masterpiece.

I encourage you to spend some more time in silence, come before God, the master builder, and ask him to show you what he sees. How does he see you? Praise God for the truth that you are his masterpiece, that you are *fearfully and wonderfully made*, that you are the *apple of his eye*. In other words, you are at the center of all he sees. Among the billions of people on earth, it's as if you are the only one God pays attention to. Being a parent

---

148   Ephesians 2.10, NIV
149   Ephesians 2.10, NLT
150   Isaiah 64.8, NIV

at your child's Christmas program, and among all the other children up on the platform, yours is the only one you notice. And, as they spot you in the audience, among all of the other parents, they relax, give an awkward smile, and a little wave just to let you know they see you too. God sees you. God knows you. God has you in the palm of his hands.

# Chapter 12

# RELEASING GUILT AND RECEIVING REDEMPTION

> "Therefore, since we are surrounded by such a great
> cloud of witnesses, let us throw off everything that
> hinders and the sin that so easily entangles."[151]

We are called to throw off that which weighs us down, hinders us, and keeps us from experiencing our peace in Christ—it could be the weight of our sin. Peace is available through the forgiveness of Christ. It could also be the weight of the guilt our sin produces that keeps us from having true peace with God and others. It's time to allow God to remove that guilt, even if there are still some residual effects.

I will get back to Hebrews shortly. First, let me talk about what it means to *batten down the hatches*. Remember, I am not coming at this as a sea or boat expert—I am not a sailor or a seaman. I had to look up what it means to *batten down the hatches*. The first thing I read was this: *prepare for trouble*.

---

[151]    Hebrews 12.1, NIV

I was reminded of Jesus' words, "In this world you will have trouble."[152] Thanks a lot, Jesus. Nobody wants to experience trouble. Jesus may as well have said, "Batten down the hatches. Prepare for trouble." I may not be a Greek scholar, but I am glad some Greek scholars have done the heavy lifting for me. I looked up the word *trouble* that Jesus uses. The Greek translation for trouble is *tribulation*. Again. Thanks, Jesus. Yes, we are going to experience trials and tribulations. We are going to experience trouble in this world. Your *trouble* will probably be different from my *trouble*.

If you are familiar with this text in the Bible, you are already probably ahead of me. I know there is more to the text. I just wanted to keep us focused on the idea of *trouble* and *tribulations*. So, yes, Jesus said we would experience troubles in this world. That's the bad news. Look at how Jesus preferences the bad news, "I have told you these things, so that in me you may have peace."[153] The good news is that despite our troubles, we will have *peace*. Jesus is preparing us, not so much for the trouble that will come but for how God will give us peace during trouble and tribulations.

Jesus said, "I have said all these things to you to keep you from falling away."[154] Unfortunately, as we know, some of the disciples did fall away, giving in to temptation. Peter denied Christ, and others did no different, even though they too promised never to fall away.[155] Judas, of course, is the one who betrayed Jesus, although, in the end, the guilt was too much for him. It is generally assumed that he took his own life. Yet, with Peter and the rest, there was redemption. After the resurrection, Jesus appeared to the women at the tomb. He instructed them to tell the disciples *and Peter* to meet him in Galilee. Jesus didn't give up on Peter, even though Peter may

---

152 John 16.33, NIV
153 John 16.33, NIV
154 John 16.1, ESV
155 Matthew 26.33-35, ESV

have given up on himself. There was redemption. Before the ascension, Jesus reminded Peter of his call—to be a fisher of men.

As I shared earlier, while in Galilee, having bone back to fishing, Jesus invites Peter to get back into the game of fishing for men and women, instead of fish. Reading further in the story, Jesus asks Peter three times, "Do you love me?" Peter, no doubt overcome with guilt, could only reply with a very weak and humble, "Yes, I love you." You probably have heard it before but let me share insight about this conversation. Jesus asks Peter three times, "Do you love me?" The first two times, Jesus uses the Greek word *agape* for *love*. Peter responds with the Greek word *phileo* and not *agape* all three times. *Phileo* is where we get the name *Philadelphia*, the *city of brotherly love*. Nothing wrong with that kind of love. However, Jesus wants Peter to be prepared for his next season in life, one that will require *agape* or sacrificial love.

Peter is aware of what he did, and he knows Jesus is also aware. Peter responds with great humility and honesty, but perhaps out of guilt, saying, I *phileo* you. Jesus meets Peter right where he's at, and on the third time, asks Peter, "Do you phileo me?" Peter can agree to that. He *dearly loves*—phileo—Jesus, but he also knows what he did. Overwhelmed by guilt, Peter is ready for the consequences, probably thinking there is no way Jesus has any use for him in building his church. Yet, Jesus assures Peter that his calling is still valid. Peter is exactly the kind of person Jesus came to earth to save. Remember, Jesus didn't come to bring condemnation, and he's not about to condemn Peter. He's going to redeem him and set Peter free from his guilt. That's what the death and resurrection of Christ has done for all of us. We too have been set free from sin and death, and relieved of any unjustified guilt. God continues to redeem us and restore us every time we fall. We just need to humbly and sincerely come before God's throne of grace, confess our sin, and receive mercy in time of need. The redeeming work of the Holy Spirit will get us back up on our feet and back in the race. God never gives up on us, no matter how much we mess things up. He redeems us, restores us, renews us, and puts us back into the game like Peter.

Jesus tells Peter, "Feed my lambs…tend my sheep…feed my sheep."[156] Peter denied Jesus three times, so in an exchange of three questions and answers, Jesus redeems Peter and gives him a fresh start. The call on Peter's life is still valid. Jesus is still going to use him to build his church. There's no time to sit around and feel sorry for himself. Jesus needs him to stop moping around and tend the sheep under his care. In other words, Jesus says to Peter, *quit sitting around in your guilt, in your shame, wallowing around in the ashes of your mistakes, and get back out there and do the work I have called you to do.*

When we are faced with trials and tribulations, and any temptation we may encounter, Jesus wants us to know that he is there for us. He meets us right where we are and picks us up, dusts us off, and puts us back on the field. Jesus redeems us, renews us, restores us, and continues to use us for God's glory and kingdom. In times of trials and tribulations and temptations, we are to cling to Jesus and draw near to him, for as he says, *in me, you may have peace.* The peace doesn't take away the troubles, overcome our tribulations, or keep us from falling into temptation. However, it is the assurance that Christ is with us. He knows what we are facing. He knows our troubles, our tribulations, and our temptations. Even if we should stumble and fall, the peace we have in him is knowing that he is with us, and he will lift us, dust us off, and get us right back in the race. Isn't that what God has done throughout Scripture with those who fell perhaps even harder than we have in our lives?

---

[156]  John 21.15-17, ESV

Knowing that we are not immune to troubles and tribulations, or even temptations in this world, we must abide in Christ, as stated in a previous chapter. It prepares us for the battles that will come our way. It's not that battles *may* come our way. Jesus said, *you* will *have trouble.* And, when troubles come, as Jesus told the disciples in the garden, *the spirit is willing, but the flesh is weak.*

Once again, in his book *God, Where Are You?* John Bevere says that the wilderness does not necessarily reveal our character, but it can produce character within us. He also says that the wilderness produces trials and temptations. Could these trials and temptations also develop our character to make us more like Christ? Jesus, while in the desert before his ministry, had his share of trials and temptations. Trials can tempt all of us to give in to the desires of the flesh. Jesus was tempted in every way we are, but he was without sin. His greatest trial was the mission that God had sent him to accomplish. Jesus faced many trials and persecutions while on earth, yet nothing compared to his having to go to the cross. Remember, while on earth, Jesus was fully God and fully human. Jesus was in the garden on the night he was betrayed, arrested, and eventually crucified, feeling the weight of the world, that is, the weight of the sins of the world bearing down on him. He struggled with the real desires of his humanity. He cried out to God, pleading with his Father to take away the burden, the weight of the cross, and the sins we placed upon him.

The darkness of the world due to humanity's sins was encroaching now upon Jesus. He was in touch with his humanity, his emotions, and perhaps aware of his fear, just as we would. Scripture says he cried out in agony to his Father, sweating drops of blood. This was the biggest trial of his life. Yet, because of being also fully God, he surrendered the desire of his flesh to the will of God.

We too may face trials and temptations on a much smaller scale. We may be tempted to give in to the desires of our flesh, to compromise, to do something immoral, to go back to old habits, back to the familiar, and back to our old life. Like our Lord, we must surrender the desires of our flesh and submit to the will of God. We find life, the life Jesus came to give when we obey the call of our Father to repent, turn from our sin, and run away from the desires of the flesh that are waging war against us. Jesus tells us to pray to our heavenly Father, saying *lead us not into temptation*. In other words, we are asking God to keep us from wandering out of His will. We are to pray for God to keep us close to His heart, and to keep us from surrendering to the lures of the world and our own selfish human desires.

We wander in the wilderness, *straining at the oars*, lost and confused.

We long for the promised land. Yet, it could be that the trials we are experiencing have caused us to fall into temptation. Yes, we may be tempted to sin, compromise our faith, skirt the truth, justify our actions, and wink at disobedience. Temptation has been part of our human existence from the very beginning with Adam and Eve. We also may be tempted to go back to our old patterns, drinking from what the prophet Jeremiah called *broken cisterns*. God says through Jeremiah, "My people have committed two sins: they have forsaken me, the spring of living water, and dug their own cisterns, broken cisterns that cannot hold water."[157]

When we turn away from God, forsaking his presence and authority in our lives, our wells go dry. Even more so, whatever we tried to fill our lives with instead of God does not last, for nothing in this world can continually give us that peace and contentment that we long for. That which we pursue in this world, instead of pursuing God, cannot hold the water we so long for. Therefore, unaware that what we need, that which we ultimately truly

---

[157] Jeremiah 2.13, NIV

desire, the presence of God, goes untapped. Whether or not we know it, we continue to be hungry and thirsty for God, longing for the living water and daily bread we once tasted, but we now do not know what to do. A saying attributed to Blaise Pascal claims, "there is a God shaped vacuum in the heart of every man which cannot be filled by any created thing, but only by God, the Creator, made known through Jesus."

Let me go back to the verse at the beginning of this chapter. "Therefore, since we are surrounded by such a great cloud of witnesses, let us throw off everything that hinders and the sin that so easily entangles."[158] To batten down the hatches is to throw off every weight that slows us down, keeping us from being obedient to God, persevering, and going forward. To batten down the hatches means we also need to eliminate disobedience, sin, and disregard for God or others that encumbers us. It causes us to trip over ourselves while running, preventing us from getting to the finish line. It is about cooperating with the Holy Spirit when we are convicted—it's not as easy as it sounds.

When we are faced with trials and temptations, it could be that we need to confess our sins; that which weighs us down holds us back, entangles us, and keeps us from running the race set before us. However, temptation raises its ugly head. We may be tempted to deny or even hide that we've done anything wrong.

When we have tripped up and have disobeyed God, there may be something that pricks us and makes us feel a bit guilty, but not enough to do anything about it. We limp along, the knot in our stomach growing, the guilt and shame increasing. We may numb it with alcohol, exercise, shopping, eating, or whatever we have to do to drown out the voice of the Holy

---

[158]   Hebrews 12.1, NIV

Spirit who is trying to turn us back to God. Or, we may be tempted to deny we have even sinned, even denying there is any guilt we are experiencing.

As we are *straining at the oars*, not making headway, painfully moving forward without results, we may not be aware that we are in the *river of denial*. "Sure, I blew it, but it's not that big of a deal." "What I did is nothing compared to what others have done." "Surely God can't be upset at me. God doesn't punish us for our sins." We so easily compare ourselves to others.

Consider the parable Jesus shares about a Pharisee who compares himself with a tax collector. *To some who were confident of their own righteousness and looked down on everyone else, Jesus told this parable.*[159] Jesus explains that the Pharisee and the tax collector had both gone to the temple to pray. So far, so good. Two praying men of God. However, the Pharisee opens his mouth, saying, "God, I thank you that I am not like other men, extortioners, unjust, adulterers, or even like this tax collector."[160] The Pharisee goes on to beat his chest, proclaiming all the righteous acts he has performed. The tax collector cannot bring himself to even look up to the heavens but humbly beats his chest, perhaps with barely the ability to pray. He says, "God, be merciful to me, a sinner!"[161]

Rather than being like the Pharisee, we should be like the tax collector. Rather than comparing our lives with the lives of others, we should compare ourselves to Christ. When we compare our lives to Christ, we realize that we will always fall short. "For all have sinned and fall short of the glory of God."[162] The *glory* of God is God's own Son, Jesus Christ, the unblemished lamb of God. Christ alone was without sin. We abuse the

---

[159] Luke 18.9, NIV
[160] Luke 18.11, ESV
[161] Luke 18.13, ESV
[162] Romans 3.23, NIV

grace of God when we freely receive God's forgiveness, that which we do not deserve, and then live our lives without realizing the price that was paid. "God made him who knew no sin (a sin offering) for us, so that in him we might become the righteousness of God."[163] As the prophet Isaiah proclaims, "he was pierced for our transgressions, he was crushed for our iniquities; the punishment that brought us peace was on him, and by his wounds we are healed."[164] The grace of God came at a price. Let us never forget that or take it for granted. "You were bought with a price."[165] We abuse God's grace when we receive his forgiveness and then live as though our salvation did not come with a price, the ultimate price, death on a cross. That is what Dietrich Bonhoeffer calls *cheap grace.* In his book, *The Cost of Discipleship,* Bonhoeffer writes, "cheap grace is the deadly enemy of the church. We are fighting today for costly grace."

The good news is that there is no condemnation for those who call upon the name of Jesus, who receive God's gift of salvation offered through the atoning sacrifice of his son. Jesus, the one who paid the price for our sins, was condemned on our behalf. "There is therefore now no condemnation for those who are in Christ Jesus."[166] The good news is that because of what Jesus Christ did for us on the cross, taking upon himself the consequences for our sins, we do not have to pay the price or be condemned. However, that does not give us the freedom to live however we want. Having been bought by Christ, we belong to God, and therefore, we are to live our lives for the glory of God. We offer ourselves as a "living sacrifice, holy and

---

163  2 Corinthians 5.21, NIV
164  Isaiah 53.4, NIV
165  I Corinthians 6.20, ESV
166  Romans 8.1, ESV

acceptable to God, which is our spiritual worship."[167] We do so not out of duty or obligation but out of gratitude for the mercies of God.

The bad news is there is still an eternal condemnation. It is for those who do not believe in the atoning death of Jesus Christ and those who do not receive forgiveness through the gift of grace offered by the sacrifice of God's son. "For God did not send his Son into the world to condemn the world, but *in order* that the world might be saved through him. Whoever believes in him is not condemned, but whoever does not believe is condemned already, because he has not believed in the name of the only Son of God."[168]

Although God may not condemn those God now calls his children, there is no free pass for anyone who deliberately disobeys God. Yet, God will and does discipline his children. "For the Lord disciplines the one he loves, and chastises every son/daughter whom he receives."[169] God will allow us to suffer the consequences of our sinful behavior, just as any parent would discipline a child. God, our heavenly Father, disciplines us not to punish us or because of his anger towards us, which sometimes earthly parents might do. God disciplines us so that we will learn and grow and mature.

You may be *straining at the oars* because of some known sin that you have not been humble enough to confess to God. It takes trust in a God who loves us to admit that we have disobeyed him. As a child, I never wanted my dad to find out anything that I did which was wrong, let alone go to him voluntarily to tell him what I did. I feared my earthly father. We are to indeed to fear God. It means we are to live our lives in reverence of Him. God doesn't want us to be afraid of Him, but instead He alone

---

[167] Romans 12.1, ESV
[168] John 3.17-18, ESV
[169] Hebrews 12.6, ESV

deserves our full devotion as we revere him, respect him, honor him, and trust that he loves us and wants more for us than we do for ourselves. We have to trust that by the death of Christ, we have been given the ability to come before God humbly. To kneel at his throne of grace, not wrath, with a contrite heart, confess our sin, and receive mercy in our time of need. We are all sinners in need of mercy, and our Father is just waiting for us to come to him to receive grace upon grace. Perhaps he is waiting for you to do just that. It doesn't mean there will be no consequences. There may be some scars left even after confessing your sins, just like the scars on Jesus after he died on the cross.

I have a little scar under my left arm from when I was a child. The scar reminds me of an event during a camping weekend with my family. One day, while on a walk, my dad and I picked up sticks and used them as swords—we pretended to be in a duel. I raised my left arm and held my stick out in front of me with my right arm to defend against my dad's lunge toward me with his stick. At the same time, I took a few steps back, like so many sword fights I saw in the movies. My left arm got hooked by a nail protruding from a tree and tore some skin off. My dad, always to the rescue, got out the first aid kit. I was impressed as he put on a butterfly bandage, and all was good. I don't know how it all happened, but the wound never healed properly—thus, the scar. My dad took the blame for my scar, although I never blamed him. He thought he didn't do the bandage right or removed it too soon. I'm sure that whenever he saw my scar, he felt guilty. We may experience wounds throughout life, with perhaps nobody to blame but ourselves. There may be scars, reminders of what we did. Every time we think of a word we spoke, an action we made, or behavior we displayed, we feel guilty. We live with regret. We can do nothing to change the past or remove the scars, but we don't need to carry the guilt. Jesus took upon himself our wounds. We are healed, set free from guilt and shame.

Jesus Christ took our sins upon himself, including all the blame, guilt, and shame that our sin produces. Out of love for us, Christ died so that we might no longer carry that weight. Christ died so that you and I might live knowing and experiencing the amazing grace of God.

Oh, we are not perfect. We still sin. We keep falling short. And, we have to admit and confess that we are *guilty* of our wrongdoings. Yet, we do not need to live with the guilt that sin produces. We will still blow it, make mistakes, disobey God, sometimes intentionally, and sometimes not so much. We will never be perfect in this world. Fortunately, God does not expect us to be perfect. Only Jesus Christ was perfect, and just as he clothed himself with our sins, so we, by the grace of God, are clothed with the righteousness of Christ. God sees us through the cross, and he sets us free by the resurrection of Christ, casting our sins as far away as the east is from the west. We will not be perfect on this side of eternity. However, God's grace is always available and ready to cleanse us of our unrighteousness. Therefore, we should approach each day aware of the fact that the ongoing forgiveness of God is still sanctifying us. We should then not only confess our daily sins but praise God for his mercies that are continually given to us every morning.

As we confess our sins, God continues to release the Holy Spirit into our souls, hearts, minds, and bodies. "If we confess our sins, he is faithful and just and will forgive us our sins and purify us from all unrighteousness."[170] As we confess our sins, the grace of God flows through us like streams of living water, restoring to us the joy of God's salvation. In one of the greatest confessions, King David cries out to God, saying, "Have mercy on me, O God, according to your unfailing love; according to your great compassion blot out my transgressions. Wash away all my iniquity and cleanse me from

---

[170]    I John 1.9, NIV

my sin."[171] Within this amazing confession, David asks God, "Restore to me the joy of your salvation."[172] Confession makes room in our heart to receive the goodness of God, cleansing us and purging us of our sins. That is the process of sanctification.

However, unconfessed sin keeps those streams of living water flowing freely through us. "If we claim to be without sin, we deceive ourselves, and the truth is not in us."[173] Unconfessed sin keeps us from experiencing the grace of God flowing through us and cleansing us. Unconfessed sin is like having a kink in a hose. There have been times—ok, several times—when I water some area in the yard, stretch the hose out, turn on the faucet, ready to commence watering, and nothing comes out. I go back and check the faucet—it's turned on. The problem is that there is a kink in the hose. I don't always learn lessons quickly, which is why I can repeat the same mistake for days in a row. Why can't I learn to first check to ensure there is no kink in the hose?

What's that got to do with anything? Let me explain.

You may have a kink in your hose—an unconfessed sin. If so, you will not experience the grace of God flowing freely through you like streams of living water. Or perhaps the hose isn't even connected to the water supply. You may have allowed yourself to become disconnected from God simply because you are too proud to admit that there is a problem. You have to stay connected to the one who gives us living water. We abide in Christ because he abides in his Father. Jesus Christ continues to be our intercessor, who said from the cross and continues to say on our behalf, "Father, forgive them."[174] As we confess our sin, Jesus Christ takes it as a sweet aroma before

---

171  Psalm 51.1-2, NIV
172  Psalm 51.12, NIV
173  I John 1.8, NIV
174  Luke 23.34, NIV

God. God, in turn releases the cleansing and healing power of the Holy Spirit into our souls. Confession truly is good for the soul. Confession releases the living waters of the Holy Spirit. It sets us free from guilt and shame and cleanses us of all the filthy, dirty, stagnant water we've been trying to survive in. Confession is God's way of having us cooperate with him. Confession will allow God to grow within us the new person and the new life, getting rid of the old, breaking the bonds of the past, and setting us free to venture out onto the high waters.

If we confess our sins, if we have a humble spirit and sincere heart as we approach the throne of God, we will receive mercy and find grace in our time of need.[175] As we draw near to him, he draws near to us, and in so doing, our hearts are kept soft and pliable. We are not only able to acknowledge our wayward ways, but we are in a position to receive the thirst-quenching, soul-satisfying grace of God. God is the potter, and we are the clay. And, as any potter will tell you, the clay needs to remain soft to be shaped.

When the clay becomes hardened, the potter applies water to soften it. Confession is a way to keep our hearts soft towards God, allowing him to release the living waters that never run dry. The disciples were *straining at the oars*, partly because it says that their hearts were hardened.[176]

If we aren't tempted to deny our sin, it could be that we are tempted to hide our sin from God or others. However, as Moses told the Israelites, "You have sinned against the Lord, and be sure your sin will find you out."[177] We cannot hide our sin because we cannot hide from the presence of God. David knew this all too well. "Where shall I go from your Spirit?

---

[175]  Hebrews 4.16, NIV
[176]  Mark 6.52, NIV
[177]  Numbers 32.23, ESV

Or where shall I flee from your presence?"[178] Our pride tries to tell us something different. We tend to believe we can hide our sins from God. The foolishness of our self-centered nature makes us believe we can hide from God. And, in trying to alleviate our guilt, to overcome our shame, we tend to flee from the presence of God.

It began with Adam and Eve. After their disobedience, "They heard the sound of the Lord God walking in the garden in the cool of the day, and the man and his wife hid from the presence of the Lord God among the trees of the garden."[179] Due to their disobedience, driven by pride, guilt, and shame, Adam and Eve tried to hide from the presence of God.

Jonah is another person who tried to hide from the presence of God. His disobedience caused Jonah to attempt to flee from God's presence. Let me stir your memory about the story of Jonah, the prophet sent by God to Nineveh. I realize that some have referred to the book of Jonah as a parable or a myth. Some believe the book of Jonah is just some elaborate fish story. However, the truth about Jonah and what took place as written in the Old Testament is based upon the fact that Jesus refers to Jonah. It's most likely that Jesus referred to Jonah as a way of foreshadowing his death and resurrection.

Jesus said, "Then some of the scribes and Pharisees answered him, saying, 'Teacher, we wish to see a sign from you.' But he answered them, 'An evil and adulterous generation seeks for a sign, but no sign will be given to it except the sign of the prophet Jonah.' For just as Jonah was three days and three nights in the belly of the great fish, so will the Son of Man be three days and three nights in the heart of the earth. The men of Nineveh will rise up at the judgment with this generation and condemn it, for they

---

178    Psalm 139.7, ESV
179    Genesis 3.8, ESV

repented at the preaching of Jonah, and behold, something greater than Jonah is here."[180]

I believe the historical events of Jonah were written down in Scripture to help us understand our history and the salvation given to us by the mercy of God. We are no different than Jonah. In our disobedience of God, we too try to flee from the presence of God. God said to Jonah, "Arise, go to Nineveh, that great city, and call out against it, for their evil has come up before me."[181]

Nineveh was the capital of Assyria, which is critical to understanding Jonah's response. Assyria was a constant threat to Israel before and after Jonah's time. At the time of Jonah, Assyria was not a threat to Israel. All was good. All was calm. All was well. Why did God send Jonah to Nineveh, Assyria, to poke the bear? Why wake up a sleeping giant? Because, as God says, their evil is known to God.

No wonder Jonah fled in the opposite direction. Who wants to be the bearer of bad news? *If you read the entire book of Jonah, there is also another reason Jonah fled from God and did not go to Nineveh. It could be that Jonah did not want to go to Nineveh because he knew that despite God wanting to call out against the evil of Nineveh, he knew that God was a God of mercy. Even though Jonah has been referred to as the Prophet of Second Chances, it could be that He did not want the Ninevites to receive the mercy of God. However, the book of Jonah is not so much a book about the judgment of God as it is about the mercy of God given to the Ninevites, to Jonah, and ultimately to us.*

Let me get back to Jonah's response to God's instructions. After God directs Jonah to go to Nineveh, "Jonah rose to flee to Tarshish from the presence of the Lord."[182] Did Jonah think he could hide from God, so his

---

180    Matthew 12.38-41, NIV
181    Jonah 1.2, ESV
182    Jonah 1:3, ESV

sin would not be found out? I tend to believe that his pride, and maybe his fear, convinced him that he could outrun God and even hide from God.

Eventually, he made it to the bottom of a ship headed as far away from Nineveh as possible and continues, "He went down to Joppa and found a ship going to Tarshish. He paid the fare and went down into it to go with them to Tarshish, away from the presence of the Lord."[183] Instead of going northeast to what is today considered Iraq, Jonah goes as far west as possible from Tarshish, which is today considered to be part of Spain. Once he got on the boat, it says, Jonah had gone down into the inner part of the ship and had lain down and was fast asleep. He did it. He outran God. He was at the bottom of a ship. God would never find him there. *Really?*

God knew where he was, just as God knew exactly where Adam and Eve were hiding in the Garden of Eden. Just as Jonah settled into the bottom of the boat, convinced he was now safe from God's presence and wrath, it says, "But the Lord hurled a great wind upon the sea..."[184] As the winds began to beat upon the ship to the point of almost sinking it, Jonah soon realized that he had not escaped the presence of God. He came to the point of reckoning. The storm, the winds, the threat facing him and the sailors resulted from his disobedience.

Once Jonah got to Tarshish and settled into the bottom of the ship, did he really think that he was out of the sight of God? *I'm thinking so.* It says that *he quickly fell asleep.* Did Adam and Eve also think that by hiding in the trees, God would not find them? Do we perhaps believe that we can hide from God or our sin from God? Do we even think we can keep it a secret from God if we do not mention our sin or acknowledge our disobedience? Like Adam and Eve, God knew exactly where Jonah was "hiding". I want to ask Adam and Eve, "What were you thinking? Did you really

---

[183]   Jonah 1:3, ESV
[184]   Jonah 1:4, ESV

think you could eat the forbidden fruit and get away with it? Did you really think you could hide from God in the garden He created?" I want to say to Jonah also, "What were you thinking? God spoke to you and told you to go to Nineveh. Why did you go in the opposite direction? Did you think you could outsmart God? Did you think he would not find you?" What about us? Do we think that God does not know where we are at all times, what we are doing, or that he does not know the condition of our hearts? Do we believe that we can keep what we do a secret from God? Do we think there will be no consequences? The truth is that no matter how hard we try, we cannot hide from the presence of God, and we should not want to. Rather than hiding our sin, hiding from God, fleeing from the presence of God, we should instead allow the grace and mercy of God to find us in our hiding. Let the love of God, poured out into our hearts by the Holy Spirit, bring us out of the darkness of our sinful nature, out of the shadows of our guilt and shame and pride, and into the glorious light of God's presence.

David knew that he could not hide from God when he said, "Where can I go from your Spirit? Where can I flee from your presence."[185] It can sound as though David was frightened by the universal presence of God. Like a teenager discovering that his parents are right there at every turn, watching his every move. Imagine, as a teenager, you go to school, open your locker, get your stuff out, close it, and there is your mom. Or, you go to the mall, and you're hanging out with your friends, and there's your dad sitting in on your conversations. It can be nerve-wracking and a bit creepy. I don't believe that is what David was experiencing. My guess is that for David, the constant presence of God was a source of comfort, assurance, and strength. No matter where David went, God was there.[186] The omnipresence of God should not cause us to be afraid or even ashamed. Rather,

---

185    Psalm 139.7-8, NIV
186    Psalm 139.8, NIV

there should be comfort, strength, and peace, knowing that God is not far off on some mountaintop but that God is with us even as we walk through the "valley of the shadow of death."[187] David proclaimed that God's *rod* and *staff* comforted him.[188]

A lot could be said about God's *rod* and *staff*, but it's mainly about the discipline and the comfort that God provides when we wander from him. The *rod* and the *staff*, God's truth and grace—read my final thoughts at the end of this book—prompts us to return to God. The *rod* and the *staff* also remind us that God is with us, and he is for us, and as the Apostle Paul wrote, "If God is for us, who can be against us?"[189] We can trust that "neither death nor life, neither angels nor rulers, neither the present nor the future, nor any powers, neither height nor depth, nor anything else in all creation, will be able to separate us from the love of God that is in Christ Jesus our Lord."[190]

The good news is this. God comes to us amid our sin, hiding, and darkness as we are weighed down by our guilt, shame, and pride. He has always come to us. He ultimately came to us in the presence of Jesus Christ, Immanuel, which means *God with us*. Remember, at the right time, while we were hiding from God, unable to draw near to God, incapable of loving God, and considered enemies of God, Christ died for us. God didn't wait for us to come to him. In Christ, God came to us. God's ultimate desire is to be with us for eternity. That's why he came to us in Christ in the first place. "For God so loved the world, that he gave his one and only Son, that whoever believes in him shall not perish but have eternal life."[191]

---

187    Psalm 23.4, ESV
188    Psalm 23.4, ESV
189    Romans 8.31, NIV
190    Romans 8.38-39, NIV
191    John 3.16, NIV

God doesn't want us to hide from him but to receive his gift of life, abundant and eternal, in Jesus Christ. The releasing of the oars is the releasing of our pride. It's also letting go of the guilt and shame that constantly plagues us. It's to come before God's throne of grace with a humble and contrite heart, acknowledge our disobedience, and receive mercy in our time of need.

In his book, *Understanding Who You Are,* Larry Crabb writes, "We're like rats scurrying about in a dark sewer, doing our best to decorate our environment with bright colors so that we can live more comfortably, then working hard to convince ourselves that we've created beauty. It is the nature of our fallenness to decline the invitation to climb out of the sewer—or to move to a beach home—to enjoy the beauty someone else has created. We trust nothing we cannot control. We think our creative powers must be used to overcome our dependence on something else, including God, so we value only those solutions that we design. Humility is not our strong suit."

May we constantly humble ourselves before God, proclaiming the simple prayer of the tax collector mentioned earlier, "God, have mercy on me, a sinner."[192] Keep in mind that mercy is defined as not receiving from God what we deserve. We are all deserving of God's wrath. We are all deserving of death. May we not receive what we deserve, but instead, may we constantly find grace, God's unconditional love, something we do not deserve, in our time of need. Take time even now to offer that humble prayer to God. As you do, receive the grace of God. Practice by simply breathing. Breathe out as you confess, even silently. Then, breathe in as you allow the Holy Spirit to renew your spirit, transform your thinking, and slowly release to you the healing balm of your heavenly Father. Allow the depth

---

[192]    Luke 18.13, NIV

of God's love to begin speaking into the depth of your soul. Allow the light of Christ to begin shattering the darkness. Allow the Holy Spirit to start chipping away at your hardened heart. God is ready to replace your heart of stone with a heart of flesh.[193]

---

[193]    Ezekiel 36.26, NIV

# Chapter 13

# RELEASING DESPAIR AND RECEIVING HOPE

"We have this hope as an anchor for the soul, firm and secure.
It enters the inner sanctuary behind the curtain."[194]

D espair is defined as the complete loss or absence of hope.

As I said before, my life verse is, "For I know the plans I have for you, declares the Lord, plans for welfare (or peace) and not for evil, to give you a future and a *hope*."[195] God's plans for us are not meant for harm but for good, to prosper us, to become who God desires us to become. It's not financial prosperity but godly prosperity. We often use this verse as though God would make us wealthy, successful, prosperous, and maybe even famous. God desires to give us a future that is filled with hope. What I have come to notice about myself is that I tend to be more focused on my past than on God's plans for my future. Sometimes life becomes so bleak that the future is hard to imagine.

---

[194]  Hebrews 6.12, NIV
[195]  Jeremiah 29.11, ESV

God wants to release us from the past, the old, so that we can step into his preferred future for our life. God knows the end from the beginning, and he calls us to trust the future into his capable hands. That is where our hope comes from. It believes that God knows our future, even when, to us, our future looks bleak. That is the essence of a faith that produces hope amid suffering and despair. We are told, "Through Him (Christ) we have also obtained access by faith into this grace in which we stand, and we rejoice in hope of the glory of God. Not only that, but we rejoice in our sufferings, knowing that suffering produces endurance, and endurance produces character, and character produces *hope*, and *hope* does not put us to shame, because God's love has been poured into our hearts through the Holy Spirit who has been given to us."[196]

In *The Power of Transforming Prayer*, J. Oswald Chambers writes, "Faith does not require external confirmation but believes God despite appearances." Hope is ours in the midst of our circumstances. Hope is not based upon a change in our circumstances. Hope is based on the faithfulness of God, who knows the end from the beginning. Hope is not based on knowing the future but on embracing the present, knowing that God is with us even if our circumstances never change.

One of my favorite books in the Bible is Habakkuk—a prophet who experienced despair. He couldn't sense the presence of God and the future looked bleak. There was nothing but *destruction and violence*. God said to Habakkuk, "I am going to do something in your days that you would not believe even if you were told."[197] If God showed us the future, would we trust it? What if the future got worse before it got better? Would it give us any hope in the present? In times of despair and hopelessness, we need to trust God with all of our tomorrows. We need to trust that God knows our

---

[196]   Romans 5.2-5, ESV
[197]   Habakkuk 1.5, NIV

future and that he holds our plans in his hands. In the meantime, we are to do as God says, "Then you will call upon me and come and pray to me, and I will hear you. You will seek me and find me when you seek me with all your heart."[198] As we begin to trust in God for the future, releasing all that keeps us stuck in despair, we need to continue to make our requests known to God. We need to pray to him, seek him, for as we release our present circumstances to him, we can begin to trust the future and receive the hope that is ours for today. Hope is not something we attain in the future, but it gives us strength for today. "We have this as a sure and steadfast anchor of the soul, a hope that enters into the inner place behind the curtain."[199]

The hope of God is the anchor of our soul in that it is immovable, steadfast against any waves or winds. Our hope is not in the ship but in the anchor that secures it. Our hope is not in the shifting sands of this world but in the steadfastness of God, who never changes. Our hope is not in one day our circumstances changing, but rather in a God who gives us confidence and certainty amid the uncertainties of this world. Our hope is secured in the promises of God, who is the same yesterday, today, and forever. Our hope is not tethered to a better tomorrow but to the God of tomorrow. Our hope is not based on the future somewhere. Hope is not merely wishing or waiting for something. Hope is here and now, available to us all day, every day.

Our hope is not in a faraway God but rather in a God who has taken up residency within us. The hope we have is safe and secure within us. It is *an anchor for the soul.* This hope "enters the inner sanctuary behind the curtain,"[200] referring to the soul. Hope is something that resides within us,

---

[198] Jeremiah 29.12-13, ESV
[199] Hebrews 6.19, ESV
[200] Hebrews 6:19, NIV

in the depths of our souls, because we have the presence of God within us through the Holy Spirit. Hope is within us—within our soul.

Dallas Willard, in his book *Renovation of the Heart,* wrote:

> "Our soul is like an inner stream of water, which gives strength, direction, and harmony to every other element of our lives. When that stream is as it should be, we are constantly refreshed and exuberated in all we do, because our soul itself is then profusely rooted in the vastness of God and his kingdom, including nature… To refer to someone's soul is to say something about the ultimate depths of his/her being."

We see the psalmist speaking to his soul in the Psalms, "Why, my soul, are you downcast? Why so disturbed within me?"[201] Then, the psalmist says, "Put your hope in God.[202] In other words, *quit hanging your head down, lift your eyes to the heavens, and trust God.* "I lift my eyes to the mountains, where does my help come from? My help comes from the Lord, the Maker of heaven and earth."[203] Where does our hope come from? Our hope comes from the Lord, the one who created us, heart, *soul,* mind, and strength (body).

Jesus tells us that we are to love God with all our heart, *soul,* mind, and strength (body).[204] We fill our minds with knowledge, even putting Scripture to memory. We take care of our bodies by having a healthy life-

---

201    Psalm 42.5, NIV
202    Psalm 42.5, NIV
203    Psalm 121.1, NIV
204    Mark 12.30, NIV

style. We tend to our heart, embracing love and giving it away, staying connected to God so that we might have compassion and empathy for others.

Our heart breaks, and we seek what we need to repair it. So, what can we do to tend to and repair our souls?

The soul is a living part of who we are, created by God. Our soul can be *downcast*, at peace, or be full or empty. Some have referred to what is known as *the dark night of the soul*. Our soul is, at times, trying to get our attention. How often do we pay attention to what is going on within us? How often do we tend to our soul?

Paying attention to our soul requires paying attention to our emotions. I'm not saying we need to *get in touch with our emotions*. It is all about recognizing that we serve a God who created us with emotions, for he is a God of emotion. Paying attention to our emotions is to pay attention to the signs that something inside is not right. It recognizes the red warning light on the dashboard. Rather than simply ignoring it, hoping it will go away, we need to do something about what this light is trying to tell us.

When we find ourselves angry or bitter, jealous, impatient, and irritated, and the list goes on, the red warning light is trying to get our attention. It tells us our soul is out of whack, drying up, and needs some attention.

In his book *Healing is a Choice*, Stephen Arterburn writes, "We are not healing our lives if we are protecting ourselves from feeling the emotions buried deep inside." He addresses the concept of actually recognizing our emotions yet doing nothing about it. In that case, Arterburn says our "lives begin to revolve around those feelings, and (we) live in a constant state of pain, hurt, mistrust, anxiety, fear and anger." Many people are *straining at the oars* because there are emotions *buried deep inside* they are either not even aware of or they simply choose to ignore. The *hope* is that they will outgrow those emotions one day or they will simply fade away. It may be too painful for many to honestly pay attention to what's going on below the surface. The truth is that it's painfully crippling not to.

Anyone who ignores their emotions may be merely surviving, "making headway painfully"[205], rather than living in the victory that is theirs in Christ. Don't ignore, deny, or bury your emotions as though you can make your feelings go away. Don't become numb to your emotions through alcohol, sex, money, gambling, pornography, and so on. Instead, admit what you are feeling and acknowledge your emotions. Share what is going on with God and trust him to help resolve it. Share what is going on inside you with trusted friends or even a counselor. Like David, speak to your soul and start asking yourself what is causing your soul to be downcast. Ask God to reveal to you what is going on inside your soul.

Suppose Dallas Willard is correct, and the *soul is like an inner stream of water*. Do we take time to soak in the living waters available to us by the Holy Spirit? Do we nurture our soul? Do we spend time listening to our soul? For our heart, mind, and strength to be alive, we need to ensure our soul receives the ingredients to produce the necessary fruit from such a well-tended garden.

I believe it is the soul that aligns the human desires of our heart, mind, and body with the righteousness of God. If our soul is neglected, everything else runs amuck. The soul communicates when things are well or when things are not right. Our soul can be filled with peace, or it can be wrought with anxiety. Our soul can have comfort, or it can be filled with fear. As David shows us, our soul can be downcast, telling us that something needs to be paid attention to. Something is trying to rob us of the hope that is ours in Christ. It makes us anxious and restless and creates a spirit of despair within us.

---

[205] Mark 6.48, ESV

Get to know your soul, have some soul time, and relish some soul food. Whatever that might be for you—reading the Scriptures, listening to music, singing, walking in God's creation, or even sitting in the stillness of a new day.

Let me go back to what we read in Hebrews. "We have this hope as an anchor for the soul, firm and secure. It enters the inner sanctuary behind the curtain."[206] The *inner sanctuary behind the curtain* certainly refers to the soul. However, it also refers to the presence of God. It was the inner sanctuary behind the curtain where the presence of God resided in the Old Testament. It was the holy of holies, where only the high priest could enter.

> *As a deer pants for flowing streams, so pants my soul for you, O God.*
> *My soul thirsts for God, for the living God. When*
> *shall I come and appear before God?*[207]

Like the psalmist, our souls thirst for God, the living God. We long to be in the presence of God. The psalmist wondered when he, like the high priests, would be able to *come and appear before God.* Perhaps the psalmist could not imagine that ever happening on earth. Fortunately, Jesus Christ, the one who now sits at the right hand of God, is our eternal high priest. When Christ died on the cross, we are told that "the curtain of the temple was torn in two from top to bottom."[208] It's as if the curtain was torn from heaven to earth, revealing that it was done by God, in the same way that God, in human flesh, Immanuel, came from heaven to earth. Jesus Christ, dying on the cross, the ultimate and final sacrifice, provided entrance into the presence of God. We can now approach God with humble and contrite hearts. Yet, with the curtain or veil of our heart being removed, God comes

---

[206]  Hebrews 6.19, NIV
[207]  Psalm 42.1-2, ESV
[208]  Matthew 27.51, NIV

into the depth of our being, giving us the Holy Spirit, who reveals to us the eternal presence of God, the *anchor of the soul.* Our hope is knowing that God will never leave us or forsake us. Our hope is found in trusting that God is with us as we are sojourners on this earth. Our hope is also knowing that one day we will be with God forever.

As Apostle Paul wrote, "For our light and momentary troubles are achieving for us an eternal glory that far outweighs them all."[209] Yes, there is eternal hope, knowing that this world will pass away one day, and we will be with our God in His eternal kingdom. One day there will be a *new heaven and a new earth.* What about today? What about now? What about hope amid our current situation and circumstances?

When I was a youth pastor, I remember a parent telling me, "*your reward is in heaven*". After an all-nighter with junior high students, this parent would say what they thought would be an encouragement. They would say, "*your reward is in heaven*". After a week away with high school students, exhausted and tired, driving long distances, barely getting any sleep, they might again say, "*your reward is in heaven*". I was thinking, that's all nice and good, but what about something here and now? What about a tangible reward, like sending me on a well-deserved vacation or a gift card to some nice restaurant?

As we wait for the day God calls us home or Christ returns, there is hope. If hope is ultimately found in the eternal presence of God, then hope is found here and now, in the presence of God, who is with us always. Since hope is found in the presence of God, who is in his holy temple, keep in mind our bodies are considered the *temple of God.* God dwells, not in some faraway place, but within our souls. Knowing that God is always with us means that wherever we go, whatever we do, we can have hope amid what-

---

[209]   2 Corinthians 4.17, NIV

ever circumstances we may face. Rather than sinking into despair, we just have to look for the presence of God.

The Apostle Paul goes on to say, "We fix our eyes not on what is seen, but on what is unseen, since what is seen is temporary, but what is unseen is eternal."[210]

We have to notice the blessings of God. We have to look to see what God is doing at the present moment. We have to pay attention to the ripples on the water, reminding us that God is at work. For the prophet Elijah, it was in a distant small cloud. We find his story in I Kings 18. When Elijah hid from Ahab during a severe famine, God said to him, "Go and present yourself to Ahab, and I will send rain on the land."[211] During a famine, God promised rain. The famine had been going on for three years—a three-year drought. Those living in California may scoff at that. Three years? That's nothing. However, when you're in a drought, especially when it comes to the soul, three years can seem like an eternity. One month can seem like an eternity. Some of you have been in a *famine* or a drought for longer than three years. No matter how long your famine or drought has been, you're looking and watching, waiting for God to do something eventually.

Amid a severe drought, God promised rain. However, the rain was not going to come right away. Yet, Elijah had enough hope to go confidently before Ahab to report the good news despite the delay. I keep hearing *"your reward is in heaven"*. It may not rain today, but one day there will be eternal showers of blessings. That's not what God was telling Elijah. It was going to rain, on earth, during a drought. Elijah could not tell Ahab exactly when it was going to rain. The good news, the hope that Elijah was clinging to and now wants Ahab to trust, was that God said he would provide rain. It wasn't so easy to convince Ahab.

---

[210]  2 Corinthians 4.18, NIV
[211]  I Kings 18.1, NIV

If you are not familiar with the rest of the story, Elijah stands against the worshippers of Baal, proving that God is faithful and trustworthy and that God's promise of rain would be fulfilled. There was to be a contest to see whose God would set fire to their sacrifice. It was quite embarrassing for those who worshipped Baal as they waited for their *god* to bring fire down on their sacrifice. Elijah taunted them, "Shout louder. Surely, he is a god. Perhaps he is deep in thought, or busy or traveling. Maybe he is sleeping and must be awakened."[212] I find it hilarious that it then says the people actually did it. They *shouted louder*. They believed that their god was asleep and they needed to wake him up. They didn't realize Elijah was being sarcastic.

After the Baal worshippers had gotten exhausted trying to wake up their god, *straining at the oars* with no results, Elijah called upon his God, the one true God, *Yahweh*. But, first, he did something a bit outlandish. Elijah had the people soak his sacrifice with water, so much so that to the bystander there was no way the sacrifice could catch fire. Yet, to the amazement of everyone, God—*Yahweh*—sent fire down from heaven that consumed and burned up the sacrifice Elijah had built.

That miraculous event convinced Ahab and the others that the God who sent fire from heaven is the God who had also promised to send rain. So, due to that display of God's power, Elijah told Ahab, "Go, eat and drink, for there is the sound of a heavy rain."[213] I am not sure Elijah heard any rain, but somehow he knew God would fulfill his promise. In spite of the drought, and in spite of there not being any rain on the horizon, for Elijah, this was not the time for despair. This was a time to hope in the promise of God.

---

[212]  I Kings 18.27, NIV
[213]  I Kings 18.41, NIV

Ahab went off to eat, drink and celebrate the good news of rain. Elijah went to the top of Mount Carmel along with his servant. As Elijah fell to the ground and prayed, the servant went and *looked toward the sea*, for the rain was coming. Hope was on the horizon. The servant went to look seven times. The servant returned to Elijah six times with nothing to report. The servant then returned to Elijah on the seventh time, saying, "A cloud as small as a man's hand is rising from the sea."[214] I know what you're thinking, it still wasn't raining, but there was *a cloud*. Sometimes, a *cloud*, a little glimmer of hope, is enough to put the wind in our sails. The cloud that the servant saw gave him hope as he returned to report the good news to Elijah.

That little cloud gave enough hope for Elijah. He then told the servant to get in his chariot and head down the mountain before the heavy rains came and prevented him from going. Elijah wasn't being a bit overzealous, reacting with his head in the clouds, or overly optimistic. He was putting his faith in the hope of the promise God had given to him.

Then, as promised, "the sky grew black with clouds, the wind rose, a heavy rain started falling and Ahab rode off to Jezreel. The power of the Lord came on Elijah and, tucking his cloak into his belt, he ran ahead of Ahab all the way to Jezreel."[215] The rain came, not just a little rain, but heavy rain. Enough to get rid of the severe famine.

What a great story, a miraculously true story, showing the power of God that should give all of us hope that one day it will rain. God is true to his word. It may not rain in our lifetime or even during our drought, but we will receive our reward one day. One day all the promises of God will come true.

Living in this world can seem like a severe famine at times. Yes, there will be a *new heaven and a new earth*. But, what about now? What about

---

214  I Kings 18.44, NIV
215  I Kings, 18.46, NIV

God giving us hope during our famine? Perhaps it's being faithful to God, showing up every day, doing what he tells us to do, watching the horizon, looking for signs, a little cloud, and reminding us that God is still involved in our lives. It's the rainbow in the sky, the encouraging word from a friend, or that unexpected check in the mail. It doesn't resolve all our problems, but it fills us with just enough hope for the moment, the day, and the season we are going through. We may never fully realize God's promise or experience hope beyond hope in this world. God's faithfulness, presence, and love are like an anchor in our souls, keeping us steady in the raging storms of life. Hold onto him as he holds onto you. There is indeed a hope that fills us and quiets our souls during the storm or famine, in times of grief and sorrow, in difficulties and sufferings.

I have realized that hope is not necessarily living by faith in the hope that things all work out according to God's purpose and for my good. Or that the circumstances that consume me will change for the better or that all things will be made new one day. What if things don't work out according to what I had hoped they would? What if my circumstances never change? How long can I merely survive until the day Jesus returns or God calls me home? Hope means that I am not just a survivor; I am a conqueror. My hope is not based on my circumstances. My hope is based on God, who fights the battle which gives me victory, despite my circumstances. My hope is based on the truth about who God is, the one who never changes, who is the same yesterday, today, and forever. My circumstances may change, but he does not. My problems may never go away, but there is hope in the one who is always with me, and *he is able*. "Now to him who is able to do far more abundantly than all that we ask or think, according to the power at work within us."[216]

---

[216]   Ephesians 3.20, ESV

God can do more than we could ever imagine possible. It makes one want to pray harder, pray more, and expect God to move mountains and part the seas. After all, *God is able*—yes, he is able. However, I don't believe that is the passage's intent, and it doesn't end with a period. It continues by saying, "to him be glory in the church and in Christ Jesus throughout all generations, forever and ever. Amen."[217] The intent of the verse is not about us believing, trusting, and hoping for God to do the impossible, but that we are to give him the glory, praise, and honor even if he doesn't. Praise God even when your mountains aren't moved, your circumstances don't change, or life doesn't get easier or better. Why? Because he is God, and *he is able* to do far more abundantly than we think possible, in ways we don't fully understand at the time. His ways are higher than our ways, and his thoughts are higher than our thoughts.[218] Our perception is limited, and as the Apostle Paul said, for now we see as though *in a mirror dimly*.[219]

We should expect him to do more than we could ever imagine. *However,* we should praise him even when our prayers don't move mountains, or God doesn't do what we expect or want. That truth is lived out by three young men in the Old Testament. You may know the story. It's the story of Daniel's friends, Shadrach, Meshach, and Abednego. *Read the story in the book of Daniel.*[220] These three young men refused to worship the gods of King Nebuchadnezzar or bow down to the golden image he created, which infuriated the king. As a result, the king ordered to have these three young men to be put into a *burning fiery furnace*. Mockingly, considering their fate, the king said, "And who is the god who will deliver you out of

---

217  Ephesians 3.21, ESV
218  Isaiah 55.9, ESV
219  I Corinthians 13.12, ESV
220  Daniel 3.8-30, NIV

my hands?"[221] What is so amazing about the faith and hope of these three young men is not that their God would save them. Rather, listen to what they said in response to the king, "O Nebuchadnezzar, we have no need to answer you in this matter. If this be so, our God whom we serve is able to deliver us from the burning fiery furnace, and he will deliver us out of your hand, O king. But if not, be it known to you, O king, that we will not serve your gods or worship the golden image that you have set up."[222] Shadrach, Meshach, and Abednego put their hope in God. They did not put their hope in God saving them from the fiery furnace. Their hope was fully and completely in God alone, who *was able to deliver* them. Their hope in God was indeed the anchor of their souls.

God is God. He never changes. We can trust who he is and who he will be, the same yesterday, today, and forever. Whether or not he chooses to intervene in our lives, rescue us from our peril, and overcome our obstacles, he is *always* worthy of our praise and trust. As a result, God receives all the glory. Our hope is in who God is, the great I *am*.

Notice what these three young men said: "*our God whom we serve is able*." They believed that God could rescue them from the burning fiery furnace. But, *if not*—if God does not rescue them from the fiery furnace, they would never put their hope in any other god. If God, the one who *is able* to rescue them from the fiery furnace, chooses not to do so, they knew that their deaths would not be in vain. God would still receive all the glory.

I have often heard that *God is God, and I am not.* God is *able* to do whatever it is we believe he needs to do. Yet, he is the potter, and we are the clay. "Woe to him who strives with him who formed him, a pot among earthen

---

[221]  Daniel 3.15b, ESV
[222]  Daniel 3.16-18, ESV

pots! Does the clay say to him who forms it, 'What are you making?' or 'Your work has no *handles*?'"[223]

You may be wondering, *why ask God to do anything in our circumstances? How can I, the clay, ask the potter to do anything?* You may also wonder what to do with verses like this: "This is the confidence we have in approaching God: that if we ask anything according to his will, he hears us."[224]

There is a condition. Ask anything *according to his will*. Sometimes when we pray, while we seek God and listen to him, we may not know what his good and perfect will is at the time. That's ok. Just pray according to what is on your heart, and God will sort it out. As you seek God and listen to him, you may discover his will, or it may be hindsight. You will understand God's answer to your prayer, even though it may not be what you prayed for or according to your preferred will. You will know that God truly is the master builder, the grand potter. He continues to bring about his masterpiece.

So, even though we don't always know how we ought to pray, we should ask and pray for God to do more than we could imagine and then wait and see what God ultimately does. Remember, our hope is not in God's answer to our prayers.

Our hope is in God, who does answer our prayers according to his will. So, why wait? Start praying. Make your requests known and begin to place your hope in the God who is *able to do far more abundantly than all that we ask or think.* Could it be that you believe God hears you, but your hope is based upon him answering according to what you pray? Is your hope not so much in God but more of wishful thinking? *I hope he hears my prayer. I hope he answers my prayer.* Guess what? God does hear you, and he will answer your prayers. God answers every prayer. It could be that you may not like

---

[223]  Isaiah 45.9, ESV
[224]  I John 5.14, NIV

his answer. You may not even want to wait for his answer. Yet, you can be assured of this, "And if we know that he hears us—whatever we ask—we know that we have what we asked of him."[225]

However, it is clear, "You do not have because you do not ask God."[226] There's a lot more James has to say about praying, but the bottom line is often we are too afraid *just* to *ask*. Could the problem be that you just do not ask God for anything, so you won't be disappointed when he doesn't answer exactly according to what you asked for? Don't get hung up on whether you are praying according to his will or that you won't get what you ask for. *Just ask!*

When my girls were little, we would go to fairs, amusement parks, Disneyland, and the like. Without a doubt, they would see something—a balloon, glow bracelets, cotton candy—and they would ask us to buy it. Knowing how soft I am, I would buy it for the girls most of the time. Sometimes I would not purchase what they wanted. Cotton candy for breakfast is not a good idea. However, I am *so* glad they asked. It would break my heart if they felt they could not ask me for anything.

Do you see where I'm going with this? God wants us to ask for anything. It would break his heart if he thought—that we didn't want to bother him or our need was too petty and selfish—we did not believe we could ask him for something.

Is there something you want, need, or lack? Just ask your heavenly Father. He already knows what we want, and more importantly, he knows what we need. Yet, as his children, you and I have the freedom, joy, and privilege to ask him for whatever is on our hearts. If we believe it's what God has put within our heart, then if we ask according to what He has put in our heart, doing our best with what we discern, we can trust that

---

[225]   I John 5.15, NIV
[226]   James 4.2b, NIV

God will answer our prayer. *Always*. Do you believe that? God answers us according to his perfect and sovereign will. We have to trust that God will answer us, not according to just what is good for us, but according to what He knows is best for us.

All we can do is pray what we believe He has put within our heart, and then trust that God can and will give us more than what we ask for. He may give us something completely different than what we asked for, but it will not harm us. God knows what will ultimately satisfy our longing more than we do. Could it be that we sometimes ask for the bare minimum? Could it be we don't ask at all? What are we afraid of? No earthly father wants their child to be afraid to come to him for anything.

Jesus made it clear, "Which of you fathers, if your son asks for a fish, will instead of a fish give him a snake instead? Or if he asks for an egg, will give him a scorpion? If you then, though you are evil, know how to give good gifts to your children, how much more will the heavenly Father in heaven give the Holy Spirit to those who ask him!"[227]

I hope that you notice two things. First, you can trust that no matter how God answers your prayers, he is not out to make things worse and certainly wouldn't give you something that would be harmful. Second, you can believe that God will give you the Holy Spirit as you pray. The Holy Spirit will then help you interpret God's answers to your prayers. The Holy Spirit is the one who can also give you contentment with what God gives you.

Here's the point. My girls may ask for a fish, and they can be assured that if I don't give them a fish, I won't give them something that will be harmful. Unfortunately, due to my limited resources, it may be tuna that comes out of a can. And guess what? They will love it. They may ask for

---

[227]   Luke 11.11-13, NIV

cotton candy at 8:00 am, and I may tell them to wait or offer an alternative, but I will give them an answer that I believe to be best for them.

Again, James says, *you do not have because you do not ask.* I encourage you to come before your heavenly Father and *just ask! Right now.* What do you want today? What do you need? What are you lacking? *Just ask!* Particularly during these times—ask God for wisdom, peace, unity, joy, and *hope.*

Our hope is not found in our circumstances—our hope is securely found in God. Our hope is not in a god on some mountain or waiting for us in eternity—our hope is in the God who is our help in times of trouble. By the Holy Spirit who dwells within us, hope floods our soul, the core of who we are as children of God and co-heirs with Christ. Claim your inheritance today.

# Chapter 14

# RELEASING ANXIETY AND RECEIVING PEACE

"Cast all your anxiety on him because he cares for you."[228]

A s followers of Christ, it is alright to be anxious, wondering where God is during our struggles and battles. Yes, anxiety is a natural emotion, but we do not need to carry our anxieties alone. As the verse above says, we need to *cast* or throw to God all our anxieties. We have to trust God with our anxieties. Without being able to give to God all of our anxieties, worries, and concerns, we will never experience "the peace of God which transcends all understanding."[229] It's a peace that will guard our hearts and minds,[230]which is where our anxieties may begin. They eventually manifest themselves in our bodies, impacting our health and possibly causing harm to our relationships. It doesn't have to be that

---

[228]   I Peter 5.7, NIV
[229]   Philippians 4.7, NIV
[230]   Philippians 4.7, NIV

way. We can trust God with our anxiety and receive peace even in the midst of our storms.

As a pastor, I find myself now and then at a loss for words. I know—shocking, isn't it? So, let me share a few words from *Eye of the Storm* by Ryan Stephenson. It's a song that had spoken to me in times when I was lacking peace. It says, *In the eye of the storm, You remain in control. And in the middle of the war, you guard my soul. You alone are the anchor when my sails are torn. Your love surrounds me in the eye of the storm.*

If you have ever looked at a satellite image of a hurricane, you probably have seen the *eye of the storm.* In the middle of the swirling clouds, there is a hole. That hole is *the eye.* Everything swirling around that whole is the storm, the hurricane. There is lightning and thunder and wind, but in the hole, in the *eye of the storm*, there is an unexplainable calm. For me, it's the image of *peace that transcends all understanding.* It's the presence of God amid the storm, holding onto me even as he battles all the chaos that surrounds me. His love surrounds me in the *eye of the storm.*

The pandemic provided a great opportunity to slow down and put things on hold because we were told to *stay home.* It's as if everything came to a standstill. However, after many days of having to *stay at home* during the pandemic, I found myself *straining at the oars.* I was not motivated to get out of bed. I became a bit weary and heavy burdened. It's not as though I had a lot of work to do. It wasn't that I found myself anxious or depressed. I just didn't know how to adjust my sails. I didn't know what *to do.* That made me anxious and robbed me of a great opportunity to experience the peace of God. I got up in the morning, went into a makeshift office in my house, had my devotions, and got right to work. That's what I was supposed to *do.* I felt guilty if I didn't *work.* If I'm honest, I was just trying to keep *busy.* I am also a person who likes routine—probably because it keeps me *busy.*

During the *stay at home* mandate, there was no routine. I found myself deleting the recurring events on my calendar. They were the things that gave me a routine. *Someone posted, 'The worst purchase of 2019: a 2020 Daily Planner.'* Without having a routine, I was finding it hard to navigate the storm of the pandemic. The shift in my routines, the *stay at home* mandate, and the inability *to do* business as usual created more anxiety than peace. I kept plodding along, taking it one day at a time because I truly did not know what tomorrow would bring. I could not *shut down*. Wanting to be a good pastor, Christian, husband, and friend, I wanted to stay busy, even by making plans for when the pandemic was over, wanting to be prepared for whatever was coming next.

Again, we are told to cast all our anxieties upon God.[231] Why? Because they are weighing us down, holding us back, and creating great confusion and angst within us. Most importantly, we are to cast our anxieties upon God because he loves us and cares for us too much to allow us to be so overwhelmed by the fears and worries of life in this world that we become paralyzed and lose all peace and hope.

One of my go-to verses had been, "Cast your cares on the Lord and he will sustain you."[232] Yes, God will sustain you and give you what you need during the storm. While in the storm, the whisper of God, the still small voice of God, continues to speak. At times it's more of a shout than a whisper. God is trying to get our attention, keeping us from fixating on the storm and the surrounding circumstances or listening to other voices. No matter what is seemingly tossing you about or even swallowing you up, God's hand is not too short that he cannot rescue you. No matter what it is that is creating fear and doubt and confusion in your life, amid the raging storms, God will sustain you, for he is with you, and he will give you peace.

---

[231]   I Peter 5:7, NIV
[232]   Psalm 55.22, NIV

You know the familiar saying, *know Jesus, know peace, no Jesus, no peace.* Without the gift of God's Son, who came into our chaotic world, filthy mess, and storms of our rebellious lives, we would never know the peace that passes all understanding and comprehension. God gave us the one who is the prince of peace. That's not just a cute title or a reference we use at Christmas—Jesus is our peace. However, keep in mind that peace is not the absence of conflict or even living without anxiety, stress, or fear. The peace of Christ is ours even when we are facing great turbulence and raging waters. It's a stillness within the storm, the presence of God himself given to us through the Holy Spirit that can quiet the pounding waves and winds by protecting us from the other voices vying for our attention. The lies and deceptions of the enemy will try to rob, kill, and destroy the peace of God within us. However, the very presence of the Prince of Peace within our soul will overcome the schemes of the enemy.

Through the prophet Isaiah, God says to us, "When you pass through the waters, I will be with you; and through the rivers, they shall not overwhelm you; when you walk through fire you shall not be burned, and the flame shall not consume you."[233] God says, **when** not *if* we pass through the waters. Therefore, we should not be surprised when we run into difficult times, face obstacles, and go through periods of great frustration, even dryness, and weariness. Isaiah says that God makes a way in the sea, a path in the mighty waters. He's the same God who divided the Red Sea and provided dry ground for the Israelites to walk upon while swallowing up those pursuing them.

When the Israelites, having been rescued from Egypt and delivered from slavery, came upon the Red Sea, it appeared as though they were doomed. If they merely looked at their situation, running into a dead end with their

---

[233]   Isaiah 43.2, ESV

enemies hot on their tail, they would have been robbed of hope. Instead, Moses looked to and listened to God and trusted that *Yahweh* would provide a way when it looked like there was no way out. Then, as we know, God provided a way, a miraculous hope-inducing way, as he parted the Red Sea and provided the dry ground to walk upon. It's perhaps a foreshadowing of Jesus, who died for our sins, who provided a way to God for all of us. We were dead in our sins, but Christ opened a way, **the way** to God, reconciliation, forgiveness, and ultimately to life by his death. The curtain in the temple was torn in two. The way for us to God was provided, as Jesus took upon himself our sin, that which separated us from God. We were facing a dead end, literally, and Christ became the *way, the truth, and the life*. There was no other way to God, to our eternal destination. As a result of the death and resurrection of Jesus, we can all come before God's throne with humble and sincere hearts. We will receive mercy and find grace in our time of need, our time of trouble, here and for eternity. God provided a way for us to have peace with him. In so doing, he will also provide a way for us to know peace in this world. The prince of peace is Immanuel; God is with us, now and forever.

When the disciples were *straining at the oars*, Jesus came walking on water to the disciples.[234]The disciples didn't recognize him. Yet, into the midst of their fears, into the midst of their storm, Jesus shows up, unnoticed at first, and speaks, "Take heart, it is I. Do not be afraid."[235] *It is I,* God in the flesh. The great *I am* is with them, right there in the middle of the storm.

Before we went into lockdown and shut down to control the spread of COVID-19, I had been rediscovering the discipline of solitude and silence—it's not that easy to practice. During the pandemic, I joined a

234   Mark 6.48, NIV
235   Mark 6.50, ESV

group on zoom that met together to share insights from Ruth Haley Barton's book *Sacred Rhythms: Arranging Our Lives for Spiritual Transformation*. In addition to discussing what we were reading, we also practiced the exercises provided in the book that helped create a discipline of solitude and silence. Those disciplines continue to be part of my spiritual transformation. I encourage you to find ways to practice solitude and silence—it takes time, practice, and intentionality. Even Jesus had to find times to get away from the busyness of life and ministry. Even when the multitudes came in search of him, wanting to receive healing, or after feeding the thousands, Jesus knew it was vitally important that he spent time alone and in communion with his Father.[236]

The need, the hunger, the longing for solitude and silence can certainly come after very productive and successful times—just go back to the story of Elijah in I Kings 18:19.[237] However, the craving to be alone and with God usually comes in a time of great distress, when we long to hear the voice of God. It's that still small voice that Elijah heard—the voice that reminds us that God is with us, even when it doesn't seem that way.

Then, as Jesus makes the disciples aware of who he is, it says that he gets into the boat, and the winds cease. As the disciples realize that it is Jesus walking towards them, they welcome Him into the boat. It was then that the storms stopped and there was peace. We need to invite and welcome Jesus into our boat, into our storms, in order to begin to receive His peace. We need to recognize that God is with us. And, although this world may change, even our lives may change, and relationships may change, or our health may change, *God never changes*. He is the great I am, and He never leaves us.

---

[236] Matthew 14.23, ESV
[237] I Kings 18.19, NIV

As Jesus said, he is with us always, *to the end of the age.* But, sometimes, we don't see him or hear him. Sometimes we wonder if he is asleep or not paying attention to what is going on in our life, world, marriage, or wherever it is. We find ourselves *straining at the oars.* Somehow, someway, we must make space for Jesus to get into the boat for the waves to cease, or at least for us to find peace and rest in the middle of the storm.

There is an episode from my childhood I will never forget. We were in Arizona, and went to Superstitious Mountain—not sure why. The name itself didn't instill confidence in me as a child. We actually ended up walking to the top of this mountain. It seemed more like a hill, but mountain makes it sound more adventurous. At some point the sky became dark. It looked like it was going to rain. We quickly made our descent and go into the van we were driving, and began to drive home. It began to get really stormy and ominous. My dad turned on the radio and heard that tornadoes were being reported in the area. He pulled off the road and into a gas station parking lot. We were sitting in the van as the winds got stronger and stronger, and the skies got darker and darker. I sat on the floor of the van behind my dad's seat. There was a sign we were parked under that began to rattle, making a loud sound due to the wind. I could see tornado funnels in the distance. I was afraid, anxious, but ironically I also at peace. Why? Because of my dad. He was sitting in the driver's seat. As a little boy, that was all I needed—knowing that my dad was with me gave me strength, confidence, and peace. I know. This makes what I shared earlier about my dad seem confusing. My childhood was actually better than my teenage and adults years.

The point is this: many people around us may not be experiencing peace in the midst of the storm, simply because they do not know the Prince of Peace, Jesus Christ. People feel abandoned and all alone on top of Superstitious Mountain. Their earthly father may not provide any kind of comfort, and they don't know their Heavenly Father. There are torna-does on the horizon, the winds are blowing hard, and there is darkness everywhere. They are filled with anxiety. Their fears are crippling them. We may not understand some of their behavior because we don't know what's happening below the surface. We may never know their pain or understand their suffering. Yet, we can empathize with them because we know what it is like when the prince of darkness tries to keep us from experiencing the *Prince of Peace*. What we can do, with the peace that we've been given, is to provide the presence of God, the peace of Christ, and the power of the Holy Spirit by loving them as Christ loved us.

We may not agree with someone's behavior or may have been hurt or offended by their behavior. Yet, God sustains us and gives us peace because he is our shield and protector and can use us to offer and provide peace to others. As Jesus bore our sins upon himself, may we receive and even carry the pain and suffering of others, not to weigh us down, but to lovingly respond with the grace of Christ. May we comfort others with the comfort God has given to us. May we also forgive others as Christ has forgiven us, for through the forgiveness of Christ we all receive peace.

# Chapter 15

## RELEASING THE FLESH AND RECEIVING THE SPIRIT

"Those who hope in the Lord will renew their strength.
They will soar on wings like eagles; they will run and not
grow weary, they will walk and not be faint."[238]

I have used this verse previously, but it bears repeating. Remember, sometimes it's just enough for you to be able to *walk and not be faint*, putting one foot in front of the other. You don't even have what it takes to run, let alone jog. You long to *soar on wings like eagles*. What does it actually mean to *soar on wings like eagles*? Is it like walking on clouds? Is it like *walking in sunshine*? Is it a time when life can't possibly get any better? Here's what I know. It's not some *pie in the sky theology*. It's a promise from God. It's about finding strength in times of great difficulty and conflict. It's rising above the circumstances than can cripple us. However, when the storms of life knock you down, it's not always about how quickly you get

---

[238]  Isaiah 40.31, NIV

back up. It takes time. You may need to learn to walk again, putting one foot in front of the other. That in itself could be exhausting. Have you ever watched an infant trying to walk? There are a lot of wobbly steps, and many times, they fall flat on their bottom while trying. Plus, before walking, there is crawling. When a baby starts walking, life for the parents is never the same. Secretly, I'm sure there are times they wished their child was still crawling.

I can't help but insert a hilarious story. It goes something like this. One Sunday morning, a preacher was giving an inspiring message. The preacher pleaded with God, "Lord, we are tired of sitting around, doing nothing. Get us up. Cause us to walk and be strong in our faith." A congregant would shout, "Help us to walk, Lord. Help us to walk." The preacher would then say, "Lord, don't let us be satisfied with walking, but help us to run with the good news, proclaiming your name to the world." The congregant once again would shout, "Help us to run, Lord. Help us to run." The preacher said, "Lord, let us not be content with running. Let us soar on wings like eagles. Cause us to sacrifice financially, giving more than ten percent." The congregant then responded, "Help us to crawl, Lord. Help us to crawl."

To *soar on wings like eagles* requires a lot of work. Nobody just decides to run a marathon. There is a lot of training that goes into it. You may want to *soar on wings like eagles,* but are you willing to do the work that is required? Are you willing to be patient as you struggle just to walk or run? Maybe it's all you've got right now to get up in the morning, put your feet on the floor, slowly move your feet, and begin walking. Perhaps it's been quite some time since you knew the exhilaration that comes with running. You just long to feel the blood flowing through your legs as you begin to walk. I'm not talking physically. I'm talking about emotionally, spiritually, and even relationally. Something has knocked you down, and you haven't been able to get back up. It's like the paralyzed man Jesus encounters at the pool near what is called the *Sheep Gate*.[239] The man had a disability for 38 years.[240] That's a long time. I don't think he ever left that spot for thirty-eight years. Thirty-eight years in the same place. Thirty-eight years as he sat and watched the waters stir and other people getting healed. Jesus comes along and says, *Do you want to get well?*[241] It seems like a silly question. But, I wonder if the person with paralysis gave up any hope of ever being healed. *Do you want to get well?* Knowing Jesus, I don't think Jesus was talking about walking. He wanted this man to *get well*. Not just physically but spiritually, emotionally, and even relationally.

I wonder how bitter this man had become over the years, watching countless people getting healed, while no one was willing to lift a finger to help him get into the water. Initially, his response to Jesus' question is, "I have no one to help me into the pool when the water is stirred. While I am trying to get in, someone else goes down ahead of me."[242] Excuses, excuses. Jesus pays no attention to his excuses. He said to him, *Get up! Pick up your mat and walk.*[243] For whatever reason, perhaps because it was the voice of God speaking to him, the man did as Jesus said, and he was cured. He picked up his mat and walked.[244] Getting up and walking was just the beginning of this man getting *well*. Yet, it began with him walking.

As you wait upon God and spend time in silence, which I discussed in the previous chapter, God will give you what you need to begin walking again. One step at a time, one day at a time, and as Isaiah tells us, you will *walk and not faint*.

---

239  John 5.2, NIV
240  John 5.5, NIV
241  John 5.6, NIV
242  John 5.7, NIV
243  John 5.8, NIV
244  John 5.9, NIV

At some point in the healing process you will *run and not be weary*. For now, you may still be weary. So, as you walk, remember to time resting in the Lord, waiting upon him to give the next instruction. Listen to his voice (through reading Scripture, getting Godly wisdom from others, prayer, silence, and maybe through a professional counselor) as he guides you into adjusting your life as you begin to run and eventually discover once again, or for the first time, the thrill of being able to *soar on wings like eagles* again or for the first time.

Peter, per his nature, wasn't always content with just being still with Jesus, or even simply walking by His side. Peter wanted to run. He was sure that he could also soar. Unfortunately, he kept tripping over his own feet. It didn't last very long for him to stumble as he attempted to walk on water. He began to look at his circumstances, and his flesh got hold of him, and he began to sink.

Peter is an example of one who kept operating according to the flesh, his human instincts, which are not always bad. He had good intentions. The other disciples were actually no different. We all want to believe we can and will do more than we are capable of doing. When Jesus told Peter that he would deny Christ, Peter begged to differ. He said, "Even though they (the other disciples) all fall away, I will not."[245] Peter went on to say, "Even if I have to die with you, I will never disown you."[246] It goes on to say, *and they (the other disciples) all said the same.* Yet, in the end, even though Peter may have been the one who denied Christ, it says that the other disciples fled, perhaps out of fear for being associated with Jesus.[247] They all fled from the scene of Jesus' darkest moment for fear of being found out.

---

[245] Mark 14.29, ESV
[246] Mark 14.31, NIV
[247] Mark 14.50 ESV

Although the disciples wanted to be strong in the moment, Jesus had warned them earlier. While praying in the garden on the night he was arrested, Jesus told the disciples, "Watch and pray that you may not enter into temptation. The spirit indeed is willing, but the flesh is weak."[248]

The Apostle Paul addressed the difference between the flesh and the spirit: "For the desires of the flesh are against the Spirit, and the desires of the Spirit are against the flesh, for these are opposed to each other, to keep you from doing the things you want to do."[249] Paul proclaims, "I have the desire to do what is right, but not the ability to carry it out. For I do not do the good I want, but the evil I do not want is what I keep on doing. Now if I do what I do not want, it is no longer I who do it, but sin that dwells within me. It's the difference between trying to live by the Spirit, but giving in to the flesh, controlled by our human tendency to depend upon our strength, our ability, and even our sense of being in control. Instead, we need to trust in God's strength, His ability to do all things, and dependent upon Him being in control of all things."[250]

How do we understand what it means to live according to the Spirit and not by the desires and tendencies of our sinful and weakened flesh? Again, Peter gives us some insight. When Peter tried to do the right thing, the good thing, he tried to do it all by himself. He was a *lone ranger* of sorts. That is not how God created us to live. Jesus told Peter, "You are Peter, and on this rock I will build my church, and the gates of hell shall not prevail against it."[251]

Simon was now called Peter. As you probably know, the name Peter means *rock* or *stone*. However, Peter, in his words, shows that we are not

---

248     Mark 14.38, ESV
249     Galatians 5.17, ESV
250     Romans 7.18-20, ESV
251     Matthew 16.18, ESV

to do our faith alone. Perhaps he learned his lesson. We are to be *living stones being built up as a spiritual house.*[252] We are to live out our faith as the church, the body of Christ, united to one another by the Holy Spirit. In the church, there are no *lone rangers.* We are built upon the Rock, Jesus Christ, who is the Cornerstone. By His death and resurrection, and through the outpouring of the Holy Spirit, we then are united together as *living stones.* As *living stones,* we are not just a pile of rocks. We are to serve together as we are *being built up as a spiritual house.* We can try to do our faith alone, and actually need times when we are alone in our pursuit of God. However, Scripture tells us not to neglect gathering together. *And let us consider how to stir up one another to love and good works, not neglecting to meet together, as is the habit of some, but encouraging one another, and all the more as you see the Day drawing near.*[253]

We cannot *stir one another up to love and good works,* let alone *encourage one another* if we are not regularly gathering with other *living stones.* In addition to that, being *living stones* means that when one of us suffers, we all suffer. When one of us rejoices, we all rejoice. Plus, to be the Church, doing the work of God as *living stones,* we will also, as individual members of the Church, be more likely to live and walk according to the Spirit and not the flesh, as we hold one another accountable.

As we are told, "if anyone among you wanders from the truth and someone brings him back, let him know that whoever brings back a sinner from his wandering will save his soul from death and *will* cover *a multitude of sins.*"[254] Also, "Brothers and sisters, if someone is caught in a sin, you who live by the Spirit should restore that person gently."[255] It is not that any of

---

252  I Peter 2.5, ESV
253  Hebrews 10.24-25 ESV
254  James 5.19-20, ESV
255  Galatians 6.1, NIV

us are more *spiritual* than someone else. If one of us is sick, those who are healthier at the time can help bring spiritual healing and restoration. It's being willing and able and humble in our relationships to *speak the truth in love* and be willing to receive it as well. That is why I propose for anyone to live according to the spirit of truth, there needs to be a connection with the body of Christ and the church. In doing so, *the gates of hell shall not prevail against* any of us.

From the very beginning, God created us to live in communion with God and one another. We were created to love God and one another. In Jesus Christ, God established the vessel for us to live in communion together. Through the death and resurrection of Christ, God established his church, the *ekklesia*. I believe God knew that we would give in to the flesh on our own. We are not capable of withstanding the devil's wiles on our own. We cannot resist temptation on our own. However, when one person sins, it can impact the rest of the body.

Ecclesiastes 4.9-12 is often used during weddings. There is a great truth for all of us to be united with God and one another, "Two are better than one, because they have a good return for their labor. If either of them falls, one can help the other up. But pity anyone who falls and has no one to help them up. Also, if two lie down together, they will keep warm. But how can one keep warm alone? Though one may be overpowered, two can defend themselves. A cord of three strands is not quickly broken."[256] These verses were originally intended to refer to how important it is to work and do life with other people.

For that reason, I want to focus on a core essential of the church: corporate worship. I want to talk specifically about how worship is our **spiritual** act. Our responsibility is to love God with our heart, soul, mind, and body,

---

256     Ecclesiastes 4.9-12, NIV

and love others as Christ loved us. I believe corporate worship is part of God's plan for us to be strengthened to then fight the battle of the flesh throughout the rest of the week. The gathering of God's people is like a training ground for us to prepare, encourage, and spur one another on to love and good works, so that we can then live more according to the Spirit than the flesh.

Early Christians were the first of God's people to be called the church, or the *ekklesia,* literally the gathering of God's people. Following the ascension of Christ, and the outpouring of the Holy Spirit, the early Christians began to live their lives and gather for worship as God's *called-out ones.* They were not just a religious group who got together once a week. They were new creations in Christ. They were deeply devoted to one another. They were deeply devoted to being together. They needed one another. They were not only committed to constantly being fed by the teaching of God's Word through the apostles, but they also longed for community and a deeper understanding of fellowship, *koinonia.*

It was a time of great persecution for the early Christians. It may have been what created a greater sense of urgency for them to be together. It could be that which we may lack in America today.

I wonder if it takes persecution, or a tragedy like the 9/11 attacks, to cause God's people to have a sense of urgency, to wake up from their slumber, and to cause a desperate need to gather as God's called-out ones. It's in times like today that we all need the Church, reminding us that we are not alone.

Gathering together is what it means to be the Church, standing together in the face of animosity, reminded that the gates of hell will not prevail against us. Unfortunately, during the pandemic, when many could not attend church, it seems to be that many Christians have gotten used to having Sundays free. They have neglected the gathering together, or they have lost the sense of urgency to gather as the Church. Isn't that what the enemy desires? Satan knows that the Church, God's people, are stronger together. Could one of his tactics be to keep us from gathering together, convincing us we do not need one another? Well, it didn't stop the early church from gathering together, and neither should it stop us.

I wonder if that is why in countries where Christians are persecuted, we hear of amazing movements of God and how the *ekklesia*, the church, is growing in leaps and bounds. In countries where Christians are not allowed to gather for worship or have a Bible study, let alone possess a Bible, that Christians risk everything to meet in secret, and as a result God is doing amazing things, like in the early Church. When the early Christians got together, in times of great persecution, a sense of awe came upon every soul, and many wonders were being done through the apostles.

It is easy for us to *do church*, to show up on Sunday mornings, put some money in the offering plates, and call it worship. It's possible to show up on Sunday, *do church*, and leave without having a sense of awe, without realizing that we were in the presence of God, without anticipating Him to do a new thing in our midst. Sunday becomes like every other day.

On February 7, 2021, some of us gathered together for worship, as we always do. That morning, I asked those in attendance to answer a question but not say it aloud. I asked, "What is today?" I'm sure some answered that it was *Sunday;* some may even have said it was *February 7, 2021*, and others who were more spiritual may have said *it was the Lord's day*. Some may have been a bit uber spiritual and thought *it was the Sabbath*. I wondered how many were thinking *today is Super Bowl Sunday. After all, it was Super Bowl Sunday.*

All those answers would have been correct. Unfortunately, that Sunday was simply Super Bowl Sunday for most people in the United States. Many fans would have attended Raymond James Stadium for the Super Bowl game between the Tampa Bay Buccaneers and the Kansas City Chiefs. When the Chiefs did something great, all the Kansas City fans would be on their feet, high fiving or fist bumping, jumping up and down, and yelling at the top of their lungs. The same would be true for the Tampa Bay fans when the Buccaneers did something worth celebrating. Why? Because for whatever reason, somehow, they are tied to their favorite teams, and for that simple fact, they are connected to each other. There is a union between those in the stands and those on the field. Even though the football game is played between the goalposts, those in the stands feel like they are on the field and part of the team.

That is what it should be like for Christians coming together on a Sunday morning for worship. When we meet in the house of God, we gather together to give our praise and thanksgiving to God, applauding His mighty works and celebrating His victories in our lives as we join our hearts, souls, minds, and bodies in worship of the One True God. As the Psalmist writes: *Enter his gates with thanksgiving, and his courts with praise! Give thanks to him; bless his name!*[257]

You and I are God's people—we are on his team. There is a union between God and us because of the death and resurrection of Jesus Christ. There is, therefore, a union between one another. We are referred to as the church, of whom Christ is the head. Jesus used that word when he said to Peter, "Upon this Rock I will build my Church."[258] Jesus was not referring to the *Church* as a building but as a group of people.

I discovered that the word in the New Testament for *church, ekklesia*, had its origin in the Greek translation of the Old Testament, the Septuagint. It was most often used to refer to the assembly of God's people. In the Old Testament, God's people were often called *the assembly*. Moses referred to

---

257   Psalm 100.4, ESV
258   Matthew 16.18, NIV

the time when the people gathered on Mount Sinai as the *day of the assembly*. The first use of the word occurs in Deuteronomy, "On the day that you stood before the Lord your God at Horeb, the Lord said to me, '**Gather** the people to me, that I may let them hear my words, so that they may learn to fear me all the days that they live on the earth, and that they may teach their children so.'"[259]

The Sabbath is to be a holy day, a sacred time for God's children to gather in His house. It's a day that is set apart for God's people to gather together to worship God. As we gather together, we are reminded that God has called us out of the world, seting us apart to be the *ekklesia*, the Church. Jesus said, "Where two or three are **gathered** in my Name, there am I among them."[260] When we gather in a church sanctuary, in the house of God, awe should fall upon us as we gaze on the beauty and splendor of God to whom we give all glory and honor and praise, as we worship God in Spirit and in Truth. I wonder if some people no longer have that sense of awe. I wonder if going to church was more of an obligation or simply a ritual. Maybe that is why so many Christians no longer attend church. It became just an activity that took place on Sunday mornings, like watching football. But as we know, the church is more than an activity or event or even a building we go to on Sundays. Church is the *ekklesia*, the gathering of God's people. So, why church? Why gather on a Sunday morning? Why have a building?

It goes back to the Temple that God instructed His people to build. God had an actual building erected to provide a place for his people to gather, to separate themselves from the rest of the world, and to be unified by God. It is in the temple that God himself was present.

---

259   Deuteronomy 4.10, ESV
260   Matthew 18.20, ESV

Remember, this is before the death and resurrection of Jesus Christ and the outpouring of the Holy Spirit. To be in the presence of God, to worship God, the people gathered together at the temple. I know you can worship anywhere, at any time, all by yourself. However, there's a reason God's people are to gather together as the Church. It's not just about the building or *going to church* on Sunday. Besides it being the Sabbath, a day God has instructed us to set aside and keep holy, a time when we are to worship God, it is also a time for us to engage in what the early Christians called *koinonia*, fellowship.

Fellowship is not attending a pot luck after church, or eating cookies in the Fellowship Hall. The actual meaning of the word we use for fellowship, *koinonia,* means to engage with one another, sharing our gifts, serving one another, as well as receiving from one another. That is why it says *that all who believed were together and had all things in common.*[261] They were selling their possessions and belongings and distributing the proceeds to all, as any had need. As we gather together, we are reminded that we are in this together and part of a larger family. By coming together, we can and should pray for, care for, and encourage one another, spurring each other on to love and good deeds. Again, we are told not to neglect meeting together, "as is the habit of some, but encouraging one another, and all the more as you see the Day drawing near."[262] We won't know how to do that if we do not spend time together. Unfortunately, some Christians believe they do not need to be part of a church family. They do not even need to worship God in some building or sanctuary.

After all, as Jesus told a woman at the well, "The hour is coming when neither on this mountain nor in Jerusalem will you worship the Father. But the hour is coming and is now here when the true worshipers will worship

---

[261]  Acts 2.44, ESV
[262]  Hebrews 10.25, ESV

the Father in spirit and truth, for the Father is seeking such people to worship him."[263] We are to worship God in spirit and *truth*. So, be honest. Why do you go to church? Is it to see your friends? Is it a knee-jerk reaction? Something you automatically do because it's something you have always done? Is it to hear good music, or a good sermon filled with great stories and jokes? Be honest, is it about the juice and cookies? Is it a time when you see yourself as an observer, and not as a participant? Is it a time for you to receive, more than to give? Or, is it hopefully to be part of something bigger than yourself? Is it to be part of that which Jesus built? Is it to renew your sense of awe for God? Is it to be able to truly engage your heart, soul, mind, and body as you love God and love others? Is it to allow the Holy Spirit to equip you as you leave the building and once again engage in the battles in the world?

So, why go to church? Why not just stay home and watch a church service on the television, listening to your favorite preacher? Let me give another reason why we need to gather together. It's the one time, and the one place, where God's people gather to share a the Lord's supper. Whenever we share Communion, it reminds us of the price Jesus paid for God's people, his called-out ones, the church, the *ekklesia*, you and me. Communion reminds us that we share in the suffering of Christ, that we might also share in his resurrection. To spend what is usually an hour a week gathered for worship with other believers is not a big sacrifice. It is essential for us to be reminded that we are in this together. We need to know that we are not alone, even in our suffering.

Let me be honest with you. Attending a church where I do not serve as a pastor is often hard for me. I tend to compare what they do as a Church to what goes on at my church. I find myself either becoming jealous or

---

[263]   John 4.21, 23, ESV

critical. When the pastor preaches, I tend to pull their sermon apart as if I could have done a better job. That can tend to be our human tendency. If worship is about what takes place up front and not what is going on in the pews, we can become very critical of what we are *watching and hearing*.

Here's the challenge for us today. When we gather together in person or online, we are not supposed to sit on the bench, merely watching what is going on. We are not to be up in the stands watching and cheering on, or complaining about, what is happening on the field. We are to be active participants in worship, not just spectators. We are to engage our heart, soul, mind, and body in every moment of our time together. Like the early Christians, we are to devote and commit ourselves not only to being together, but we are to actively be involved in what is going on as we listen to the word of God. We are to engage in fellowship, caring and serving those around us. We are to be encouraging one another. We are to be available to pray for one another, rather than just listening to a prayer offered from up front. We can and should be praying throughout the entire service, asking God to pour out his Spirit upon us, giving us a sense of awe, allowing ourselves to be inspired by God to go forth as His disciples. Keep in mind, worship doesn't end when we leave the building. God doesn't wave good bye to us, saying, "See you next Sunday." He goes with us. Our worship, like prayer, should be done without ceasing.

As we know, the early Christians gathered together in each other's homes *daily*. Worship is not something we do just on a Sunday morning. We engage in worship wherever we are, and in whatever we are doing. A sense of awe can fall upon us in the sanctuary, and as we look for and experience the presence of God every day of the week. We are to seek him daily, drawing near to him, worshipping him, aware of his presence with us in all that we do. We are still the church when we are at work, school, or in our neighborhoods. We are to represent God to the world. We are to be ambassadors for Christ. We are to be salt and light in the world. It's not about being moral police, but living as the people of God, the Church, in all we do or say. A pandemic make prevent us from being together, but it cannot stop us from being the Church.

In a time of great persecution, nothing and nobody could keep the early Christians from being the Church. They not only gathered in the Temple once a week, but they met together in homes during the week. Fortunately, or perhaps unfortunately, we are not facing the type of persecution the Early Church endured. We are able to gather together without fear of persecution. Let's not take that for granted. Remember, *ekklesia* means the assembly or gathering of God's people, the called-out ones, set apart from the world. When applied to the church in the New Testament, *ekklesia* carries the Old Testament definition of standing together as God's chosen people.

That is still our calling today. We are to still gather together as the *ekklesia* partly in order to be reminded that God has set us apart from the world. It's about us representing God—the Father, Son, and Holy Spirit—not just on a Sunday morning but every day and every moment of every day. It's not about social distancing. It's about a holy gathering. The church, the gathering of God's people, reminds us that we may in the world, but we are not of the world. I read something that said, "A local church is an assembly. If a church never meets, it is no church at all. Meeting, however, isn't just something churches do. A meeting is, in part, what a church is. God has saved us as individuals to be a corporate assembly. It's not what we do. It's who we are."[264]

---

[264]  Anonymous.

## *Chapter 16*

# RELEASING BURDENS AND RECEIVING REST

"Cast your burden on the Lord, and he will sustain you;
he will never permit the righteous to be moved."[265]

**Y**ou can give your burdens to God, trust Him with your burdens, knowing that God will sustain you. Whatever it is that might be weighing you down, God will give you what you need so that you are not *moved*, destroyed, or overwhelmed by the burdens of your life in this world. Jesus knows your burdens, because He carried them to the cross. He bore your burdens. He knows you are weary. He also was weary as His impending death was on the horizon. It's no wonder Jesus said, "Come to me, all you who are weary and burdened, and I will give you rest."[266]

Notice that Jesus didn't say *you will have rest*. He said *I will give you rest*.

God knows exactly what we need. Sometimes what we need is a time of rest. It could be just a nap, although the *rest* that Jesus gives us refreshes

---

[265]  Psalm 55.22, ESV
[266]  Matthew 11.28, NIV

our soul, not just our body. As David realized, sometimes God makes us rest when we can't do it for ourselves. Knowing God as his Great Shepherd, David proclaimed, "He makes me lie down in green pastures, he leads me beside quiet waters, he refreshes my soul."[267] God longs to give us rest in the midst of our busy and chaotic lives. He also longs to refresh or restore our souls in our times of suffering.

How does God provide or give rest to the weary? Look at what God says through the Prophet Isaiah, "When you pass through the waters, I will be with you; and when you pass through the rivers, they will not sweep over you. When you walk through the fire, you will not be burned; the flames will not set you ablaze."[268] Notice that it's not *if*, but *when you pass through the waters*. When we pass through the waters, or the storms, God promises to be with us to protects us. God is with us in a dry and weary land.

We should not be surprised when we run into difficult times, face obstacles, and go through periods of great frustration, even dryness, and weariness. The Apostle Paul was certainly aware of life's difficulties, "We are afflicted in every way, but not crushed; perplexed, but not driven to despair; persecuted, but not forsaken; struck down, but not destroyed; always carrying in the body the death of Jesus, so that the life of Jesus may also be manifested in our bodies."[269] Paul did not deny the suffering he experienced. Yet, he trusted that God would protect him and give him life in Jesus, the one who gives us our help and rest in a time of need.

Jesus told the disciples, "In this world, you *will* have troubles."[270] Jesus also said and promised that he has and will overcome all troubles. Yes, we

---

267    Psalm 23.2b-3a, NIV
268    Isaiah 43.2, NIV
269    2 Corinthians 4.8-10, ESV
270    John 16.33, NIV

*will* have difficulties, troubles, and trials, but God will see us through them. He will provide a way for us through the fires and the floods.

When the Israelites were fleeing from the Egyptians, they came upon the Red Sea. It appeared as though they were doomed. There was nowhere to go. There was no *way* for them to survive their enemies. But, as we know, God parted the seas and provided a way. Jesus, who died for our sins, provided the ultimate way for us all. We were dead in our sins. There was nothing we could do to find our way to God. We could not, in our own strength and power, create a way to have eternal life with God. Christ, by his death, opened a way, *the way* to God, to reconciliation, to forgiveness, and ultimately to life, abundant and eternal. When Jesus died on the cross, Scripture tells us that the curtain in the temple was torn in two. The curtain that once divided God from His people, was ripped from top to bottom. By the sacrificial death of Christ, we now had access to God's throne of grace. It wasn't the curtain in the Temple that separated us from God. It was our sin. Jesus took not only our burdens upon Himself, but He took our sins upon His body. We can all come before God's throne with humble and sincere hearts and receive mercy and find grace in our time of need. Being reconciled to God through the death and resurrection of Christ allows us to also receive rest for our souls. We have a sure hope of being present with God for eternity. Our burdens are lifted as we confess our sins, trusting and believing that God will not only forgive us, but that He will "cleanse us from all unrighteousness"[271] Our current earthly burdens do not compare to the burden that Jesus carried for us on the cross, as He who knew no sin became sin on our behalf, "so that in Him we might become the righteousness of God."[272]

---

[271]  I John 1.9, ESV
[272]  2 Corinthians 5.21, ESV

God has provided *the way* for all of us to have life for eternity and abundantly here. We do not need to wait until we are with God in his kingdom to find rest. God will provide a way for you to receive rest even in the wilderness you might be experiencing right now. "I will make a way in the wilderness and rivers in the desert."[273] Even in times of great trouble and weariness in the desert, God is making all things new. He is at work, even if we may not *perceive it.* He is indeed making *a way in the wilderness and rivers in the desert.* No matter what we go through in this life, even death itself, God is with us, and we *fear no evil.* We will overcome, and God will give us the victory. He brings beauty out of ashes, joy out of sorrow, and life out of death. "For I will pour water on the thirsty land, and streams on the dry ground; I will pour my Spirit upon your offspring, and my blessing on your descendants. They shall spring up among the grass like willows by flowing streams."[274]

As we put our faith, hope, and trust in the one true God, he *will* give us new life and rest. Too often, though, we are so busy that we don't have time to be still and *rest.* God may have to make us rest literally and physically. He may have to cause us to *lie down in green pastures* or *lead us beside quiet waters* to *refresh* or *restore* our souls. He might create a *famine*, a season when there is nothing we can do but find our rest in him. It could be a physical illness, unemployment, divorce, financial despair, a broken relationship, or anything that will cause us to stop, be still, and turn to him to find the rest we need. So, don't wait until God has to cause you to stop your running around.

Remember Martha? She was someone who just could not *rest*—she was a busy body. You know the story about Jesus coming to her home, where she lived with her sister Mary. I'm not going to berate Martha because I

---

[273]  Isaiah 43.19, ESV
[274]  Isaiah 44.3-4, ESV

feel I would have done the same thing. Like Martha, I would have wanted to make things ready to welcome Jesus. I may have answered the door, saw him standing there, and then closed the door to straighten things up. Unlike Martha, Mary welcomed Jesus into her home, no matter the condition. It's not that Martha did anything wrong. She was *distracted* and she was *distracted with much serving*. Shouldn't we all be serving Jesus and others? Unfortunately, she was about to miss out on a great opportunity. As Jesus correctly discerned, Martha was *anxious and troubled about many things*.[275] She was *straining at the oars*, serving Jesus, or perhaps wanting to please Jesus. Jesus wanted her to sit with him and chat, like her sister Mary was doing. She needed to put down the oars, put down her anxieties and troubles, and rest at the feet of Jesus. That is what Jesus said was, at the moment, *the one thing necessary* for Martha to do. After all, Jesus came to serve, not to be served. Mary, according to Jesus, *chose the good portion*, perhaps the right thing at the right time.

So, right now, I want you to spend time at the feet of Jesus. I dare you; I double-dog dare you. Go ahead and try to spend five minutes in silence—right now. Go ahead, stop reading, and sit in silence for *five minutes*. Sounds easy? Give it a try. Before you do it, let me remind you that as you seek that sweet spot, the *eye of the storm*, giving access to God during some of life's most difficult and stressful times, it can also be risky. Remember, the *eye of the storm* can be the most peaceful place, but it can also be the least safe place. As you spend time alone, in silence, allowing God to whisper into your storms, there may be some things that are revealed that may not be pleasant. As the Holy Spirit is given access into your soul, that which has been hidden for a lifetime may soon surface for God, the healer, the great physician, in order to begin the necessary surgery to set you free and give

---

[275]   Luke 10.41, ESV

you unbelievable peace. Try to allow yourself to invite God into your storm to create some space for the Holy Spirit to begin blowing away the cobwebs before you read on. If you are able, try to go longer than five minutes.

Did you make it? Did it seem like an eternity? What did you find yourself thinking about? What were you made aware of? Emotions? Things to do? Worries? Now take time and write down what you experienced in those five minutes.

Did you do it? Did you write it down? Good. Now, spend another five minutes in silence, trusting God with all you wrote down. This time, ask God to tell you what he has for you and listen in silence. Ask him to show you an image, a vision, a word, or a Scripture. Don't say anything. Just *listen*. Sounds easy? Give it a try—five minutes.

I hope you did it. God is with us always. Sometimes, when there is so much going on around us, a variety of voices speaking to us, telling us what to do, how to act, what to trust, the one true voice can get lost. During the storm, we can easily be robbed of the peace that truly does occur in the presence of God. A quiet peace. A confident peace. A certain peace. Silence is golden—it's a treasure, a gift.

> ➤ Even a fool who keeps **silent** is considered wise; when he closes his lips, he is deemed intelligent.[276] (A friend of mine said that Job's friends were great—until they opened their mouths.)
> ➤ And when you pray, do not heap up empty phrases as the Gentiles do, for they think that they will be heard for their **many words**.[277]
> ➤ Be **still**, and know that I am God.[278]

---

276  Proverbs 17.28, ESV
277  Matthew 6.7, ESV
278  Proverbs 46.10, ESV

- ➢ For God alone my soul waits in **silence**; from him comes my salvation.[279]
- ➢ For God alone, O my soul, wait in **silence**, for my hope is from him.[280]
- ➢ When the Lamb opened the seventh seal, there was **silence** in heaven for about half an hour.[281]
- ➢ Be silent, all flesh, before the LORD, for he has roused himself from his holy dwelling.[282]

Sometimes there are no words to say—nothing to do—just silence and stillness before the Lord—waiting for him to speak—to breathe into our lungs and fill us with new life.

---

[279] Proverbs 62.1, ESV
[280] Proverbs 62.5, ESV
[281] Revelation 8.1, ESV
[282] Zechariah 2.13, ESV

# FINAL THOUGHTS

E ventually you will be rowing again, but hopefully not in your strength. Perhaps you are already rowing—steady as it goes. My prayer is that you have realized you cannot do it alone. Hopefully, you realize you cannot become the person God knows you already are by using your strength, your wisdom, or setting your course without him. As *co-laborers* with Christ, it will be necessary for you to take responsibility for what you can and should do and what you are not supposed to do. You will need to put the two oars back into the water and begin to row, guided by the Holy Spirit, with the presence of God and in the name of Christ. The two oars that I want to suggest you continue to use are *grace* and *truth*.

We must row with both oars. We cannot row with one and not the other. We must row with truth *and* grace. They are the nature and person of Christ. "The Word became flesh and made his dwelling among us. We have seen his glory, the glory of the one and only Son, who came from the Father, full of grace and truth."[283] It is the grace of God that sent Jesus into our world and into our lives to save us. It is the truth of Christ that has set us free. The Holy Spirit continues to use grace and truth to redeem us and restore us and rebuild us throughout our journey in this world.

---

[283] John 1.14, NIV

The big obstacles for many of us trying to get to where God leads us are the lies and deceptions of our flesh, humanity, this world, and the enemy, *the father of lies.* So many times, our battle is not against that which is tangible, or as Paul says, *flesh and blood.* Paul writes, "For our struggle is not against flesh and blood, but against the rulers, against the authorities, against the powers over this dark world and against the spiritual forces of evil in the heavenly places."[284] Our struggle, our battle, is, at times, not something we may always recognize. It may not be something we can put our finger on. That's because we are at war at times against the *spiritual forces of evil.* I'm not suggesting we look for the devil under every rock or around every dark corner. However, I wouldn't ignore the fact that the devil does exist. In mentioning Satan, Jesus says, "he is a murderer from the beginning, and does not stand in the truth, because there is no truth in him. When he lies, he speaks out of his own character, for he is a liar and the father of lies."[285] Satan lies and deceives. It is his nature. It is what he does. He doesn't just distort the truth—*he lies.* He will whisper in your ear and tell you that God does not love you. He will try to convince you that you are not *doing* good enough or are not *doing* any good. He will beat you down and convince you that your sins are not forgiven, not just what you did today, but what you did years ago. In his devotional *Encountering the Goodness of God,* Bill Johnson writes, "Entertaining a lie is a poison that works into our being to destroy our identity and purpose." Satan will try to convince you that you are defined by your past. Jesus' death delivers you from the past. We are *new creations in Christ.* Satan is the antithesis of Jesus. Jesus is full of grace and *truth.* Jesus came to give us an abundant and eternal life. Satan wants to keep us from experiencing that life. He does that by filling us with lies.

---

284 Ephesians 6.12, NIV
285 John 8.44, ESV

The grace and truth of Jesus sets us free as we receive the mercy and forgiveness of God. So, instead of listening to the lies of Satan, the one who wants to convict and condemn, we need to approach God's "throne of **grace**, with humble and sincere hearts, that we may receive mercy and find **grace** to help in time of need."[286] The enemy cannot take away the grace and truth that is ours in Christ. The grace of God assures us of the truth, that the death of Christ has provided us the forgiveness for our sins. The enemy wants to condemn us and define us by our past. Satan wants to paralyze us by guilt and shame. On the other hand, "God did not send his Son into the world to **condemn** the world, but so that the world might be saved through him."[287]

Jesus came to set us free with grace and truth. As Jesus said to the woman caught in adultery, "Has no one condemned you?... Neither do I condemn you; go, and sin no more."[288] The truth of Christ, the truth that none of us is perfect, is not meant to condemn us. Instead, the truth is meant to convict us, cause us to turn to God, receive mercy, and find grace in our time of need. The truth is given so we might repent and confess our sins, trusting and believing that as we do, God "is faithful and just to forgive us our sins and to cleanse us from all unrighteousness."[289] It is God's kindness, his grace, not his wrath or his anger or even his condemnation, that leads us to repentance.[290] *Therefore,* the Apostle Paul assures us, "There is therefore now no condemnation for those who are in Christ Jesus... He who did not spare his own Son but gave him up for us all, how will he not also with him graciously give us all things? Who shall bring any charge against God's

---

[286]   Hebrews 4.16, NIV
[287]   John 3.17, ESV
[288]   John 8.10-11, ESV
[289]   I John 1.9, ESV
[290]   Romans 2.4, ESV

elect? It is God who justifies. Who is to condemn? Christ Jesus is the one who died—more than that, who was raised—who is at the right hand of God, who indeed is interceding for us."[291]

***Christ took our condemnation upon himself.***

So, how do we combat the lies the enemy wants to use in order to condemn us? Paul says, "Therefore take up the whole armor of God, that you may be able to withstand in the evil day, and having done all, to stand firm."[292] As we put on the armor of God, we are able to stand against the lies of the enemy with the Truth of Jesus Christ, who is the Word of God made flesh. Therefore, the Truth of Christ is found also in God's written word. As Jesus said, the truth will set us free if we abide in his word, which is the way we abide in him. In God's word, we find the Truth, for it is the Word of God that tells us about the one who came to set us free, the one who is full of *grace* and *truth*. It's in the *truth* of God's word that reminds us of the goodness of God. It is where we also encounter the truth about who we are when we strive to live apart from Christ. The enemy wants us to remain apart from Christ. He does so by trying to rob us of our identity in Christ.

This final chapter came to me while going through difficult transitions in life and ministry. I was clinging to the *grace* and *truth* of who I was in Christ as I began to realize that I had been *straining at the oars* of approval and acceptance of others, which comes from *straining* not wanting to disappoint anyone or let them down. Not that I was hardening my heart to the views and opinions of others. Rather, I was learning to release oars that were robbing me of God's *grace* and *truth*. I slowly began *straining forward* in order to live more consistently with who I am in Jesus Christ. I began putting on the full armor of God in order to combat and resist the lies of

---

[291]  Romans 8.1, 32-34, ESV
[292]  Ephesians 6.13, ESV

the enemy who was trying to keep me from being the person God longs for me to become. I know that my Father sees me not just as I am, but as the person he is transforming me into by the power of the Holy Spirit.

As I begin to *strain forward,* knowing that there will still be storms that rage against me, I am clinging to the *grace* and *truth* of Christ as God brings beauty from ashes. I am trying to discover my own spiritual rhythms, as I carefully set down the oars of guilt and shame, and learning how to rest in the *grace* and *truth* that are mine in Christ. I am trying to live in the moment, one day at a time, trusting and believing that the mercies of God are new every morning. I am learning to believe the truth that Jesus came not to condemn me, but in order to save me, rescue me, and reconcile me to my heavenly Father as he continues to restore my identity as a child of God. I remain in the smoldering *ashes* of my old self, even as God begins to provide a the way forward. He sustains me. He meets me every morning and is with me every step of every day. That's not to say that there aren't difficult days and difficult choices to be made along the way. Still, God gives me what I need every day so that I can leave the *wilderness* behind as he leads me into the *promised land.* He keeps my heart from becoming hardened so that I might receive the new wine he gives to me daily.

In the devotions that prompted this chapter, I was reminded that Jesus came to give me life. Yes, life eternal, which nothing can compare. However, Jesus came to give me and you an abundant, rich, blessed life, here and now, that nobody nothing can take away from us. The enemy, as we know, will try very hard to rob, kill and destroy all that belongs to us from God. However, nothing, not even the enemy's attacks, can keep us from receiving the abundant life that is ours in Christ through the outpouring of the Holy Spirit. That is what is so rich about the gift of Communion, the Lord's Supper, shared with other believers. Those who put faith in Christ are invited to regularly come to the table to receive the bread and the wine—juice for most of us. The invitation is made to all who believe or choose Christ at that moment. It is not a table of condemnation but a table of grace and truth that reminds us of God's forgiveness. It is a table of refreshment, where the grace and truth of God meets us in our deepest and darkest needs. Jesus tells us that when we eat the bread and drink from the cup, we are to do so in remembrance of Him. We are to remember the sacrifice of Christ, not our sins that sent Him to the cross. We are to remember the grace of God given to us through the Holy Spirit, not the condemnation that comes with guilt. As you read the following, I invite you to come to the table to eat and drink of the goodness of God.

Reading in Bill Johnson's *Encountering the Goodness of God*, I was prompted to sit and be still and allow the Holy Spirit to help me recall the goodness of God. Listed below is what the Holy Spirit showed me, that I hope blesses you. I encourage you to read my words and, most importantly, read the Scripture passages. At the end of your reading, spend time in silence listening to God. Allow the Holy Spirit to reveal to you the goodness of God for today and for all your tomorrows. Here is the goodness of God revealed to and claimed by me, that I hope refreshes your soul as well:

1. God is my *provider.* I have not lacked anything throughout my life, and I need not fear that I will lack anything today or in the future. The obvious verses that come to mind are the words of Jesus, reminding me that I do not need to be anxious about my provisions in this life, for God will give me what I need, for he alone knows what I *need.*[293] He takes care of the birds. How much more will He take care of me? Another Scripture to consider is, "Every good gift and every perfect gift is from above, coming down from the Father of lights, with whom there is no variation or shadow

---

[293] Matthew 6.31-32, ESV

due to change."[294] My circumstances may change, but God remains faithful. He is the same yesterday, today, and forever. Great is his faithfulness.[295]

2. God is my *healer.* God is the great physician. However, it's not just physical healing he can provide. He is capable of emotional healing. I know that I will be completely healed of every infirmity and affliction even at my resurrection. It's just not the physical healing that God provides. He brings healing to my soul, heart, mind, and spirit. By the blood of Christ, we have been *healed,* made right with God, which allows us to receive the healing that comes from the Holy Spirit. "He was pierced for our transgressions; he was crushed for our iniquities; upon him was the chastisement that brought us peace, and with his wounds **we are healed**."[296]

3. God is my *sustainer.* God knows what I need to sustain me better than I do. "Cast your burden on the Lord, and he will sustain you."[297] I will continue telling God what I believe I *need, want* and *desire,* but I then need to allow him to reveal to me how he has given me what I truly *needed.* I need to pay attention to how God gives me exactly what I need at the moment. I am trying to sit with God long enough in order to pray for what He puts on my heart, what He knows I need, rather than me just telling him what I want. I am trusting that God will give me the desires of my heart, that which He desires for me.

4. God is my *redeemer.* Job, the person who knows what it is like to lose everything, and I mean everything, proclaimed these amazing

---

294 James 1.17, ESV
295 Lamentations 3.23, NIV
296 Isaiah 53.5, ESV
297 Psalm 55.22, ESV

words, "For I know that my **Redeemer** lives, and at the last he will stand upon the earth."[298] God will indeed make all things new, redeeming that which has been lost or broken. "The Lord redeems the life of his servants; none of those who take refuge in him will be condemned."[299] "I have blotted out your transgressions like a cloud and your sins like mist; return to me, for I have redeemed you."[300] God has purchased us with the blood of Christ. We no longer need to live broken lives, lost in the wilderness, or even stay in the ashes of our guilt. We can rise and turn to God, follow his voice as he leads us out of the ashes, out of the desert, for he has redeemed us. We belong to him, and our identity is in him. We are not defined by our failures, brokenness, wounds, or even our sins. We are defined by who we are now as children of God, redeemed and ransomed by our Savior, Jesus Christ.

5.   God is my *restoration*. God restores as He brings beauty of ashes God heals the brokenhearted. He takes us as we are, the good, the bad, and the ugly. Fortunately, that is not where he leaves us. Due to our sinful nature that was birthed back in the garden, we are a people in need of restoration. We need God to restore us to who we were, the person God knew we were before we were ever conceived. To be restored is to be made whole. In this world we will always be incomplete, but by the goodness of God, we can be made whole. We can be holy and righteous, because we have been made clean by the blood of Christ. We are broken vessels, but God is not done with us. Unlike our western culture, where broken things are thrown away, God takes our broken lives and restores us

---

298   Job 19.25, ESV
299   Psalm 34.22, ESV
300   Isaiah 44.22, ESV

into his image. We will experience full restoration when we are in our Father's kingdom. Notice how God is already beginning the restoration process. God says, "Behold, I am **doing** a new thing; **now** it springs forth, do you not perceive it? I will make a way in the wilderness and rivers in the desert."[301]

As God restores you, he also renews you and makes you even better and stronger than before. There may be a time, even a season of affliction and brokenness, but God will renew and rebuild and restore you. "And after you have suffered a little while, the God of all grace, who has called you to his eternal glory in Christ, will himself **restore**, confirm, strengthen, and establish you."[302]

Even in the book of Lamentations, the author, filled with so much sorrow due to afflictions, cries out to God, "Restore us to yourself, O Lord, that we may be restored!"[303] Ask God to restore whatever is broken that appears unrepairable or irredeemable.

6. God is my *refuge*. He is my hiding place. This is not just about Corrie Ten Boom or a song we sang around the campfire. It's a truth we need to proclaim, "You are a **hiding place** for me; you preserve me from trouble; you surround me with shouts of deliverance."[304] The greatest place to run when trouble comes is into the arms of our Lord. The reality is that he never lets go of us. We are always in his embrace. Consider these words, "How precious is your steadfast love, O God! The children of mankind take refuge in the shadow of your wings."[305] What a great image. Maybe take

---

[301]  Isaiah 43.19, ESV
[302]  I Peter 5.10, ESV
[303]  Lamentations 5.21, ESV
[304]  Psalm 32.7, ESV
[305]  Psalm 36.7, ESV

time to feel the embrace of God wrapping his arms around you, sheltering you, protecting you. He is your shield. When this world beats you up, he will protect you and provide a way through whatever storms you face. When people speak negatively of you, when rumors and gossip swirl around destroying your character, God will be your defense. You don't even have to say a word. As Jesus hung on the cross, and people were hurling offensive words and insults at him, he remained silent, for he knew his Father would defend him. And, three days later, that is what God did.

7. God is my *rescuer*. He sent his son, Jesus Christ, to rescue you and me. God sent his Son as the ultimate search and rescue party to redeem and rescue us. Jesus came to *seek and save the lost*.[306] God has been described as the *hound of heaven*. As the *good shepherd*, Jesus leaves the 99, those who are safe and secure, and he goes after the one lost sheep, the one that is in trouble as it wanders from the rest of the flock. Praise God that he has rescued you and and that He will continue to rescue you. When you feel lost and alone, proclaim, "The Lord will rescue me from every evil deed and bring me safely into his heavenly kingdom. To him be the glory forever and ever."[307]

8. God is my *renewer*. "So we do not lose heart. Though our outer self is wasting away, our inner self is being renewed day by day."[308] Because of the above points, I believe that when I am weak, God will renew me—heart, soul, mind, and body. Part of our restoration is the renewal of our minds. He can take our thoughts, the ones that lead us astray, the ones that put us in a downward spiral,

---

[306] Luke 29.10, ESV
[307] 2 Timothy 4.18, ESV
[308] 2 Corinthians 4.16, ESV

even the enemy's lies, and by his truth, set us free from even our most hurtful self-talk. God renews our mind as He changes the way we think. Consider, "For the weapons of our warfare are not of the flesh but have divine power to destroy strongholds. We destroy arguments, and every lofty opinion raised against the knowledge of God and take every *thought* captive to obey Christ."[309]

Part of the enemy's tactic is to gain control of our thoughts. Not just filling us with impure thoughts but with self-defeating thoughts. That is a powerful weapon. We need to constantly recognize those thoughts, give them to God and ask him to reveal his thoughts and his truth to us. Ask God to plant truth within your mind. Ask God to protect your thoughts from taking you down the wrong path. "Lead us not into temptation, but deliver us from evil."[310]

Ask God to protect your mind from the attacks and deceptions of this world so that you can withstand the devil's wiles and begin to fix your thoughts on that which is of God. "Do not be conformed to this world, but be transformed by the renewal of your mind, that by testing you may discern what is the will of God, what is good and acceptable and perfect."[311] "Set your **minds** on things that are above, not on things that are on earth."[312]

9. God is my *refiner*. To be refined means that we may have to go through the *refiner's fire*[313]. I landed upon another term that I have referred to—the *furnace of affliction*. "Behold, I have refined you,

---

[309] 2 Corinthians 10.4-5, ESV
[310] Matthew 6.13, ESV
[311] Romans 12.2, ESV
[312] Colossians 3.2, ESV
[313] Malachi 3.2, ESV

but not as silver; I have tried you in the **furnace of affliction**."[314] We all want to be restored, renewed, rescued, and refined. None of us wants to go through the fire. None of us wants to experience the *furnace of affliction*—it is painful. But there first need to be ashes for there to be beauty. That has become a new revelation for me.

God does not bring beauty out of beauty. He brings beauty out of ashes—ashes don't seem useful for anything. God sees it differently, and it's in the ashes that he does his greatest work. It's in the *furnace of affliction* and through the *refiner's fire* that God brings about a new creation. Don't avoid the furnace or the fire. Don't deny the pain of affliction. Don't ask, "Why God?" Instead, ask, "What?" "What are you going to do with this God?" "What do you want me to learn during this time, God?" Remember, *no pain, no gain. Ok, not the best analogy.* It's just that suffering and pain are not always bad.

Let me end with something I learned from Matthew Kelly's book *Life is Messy*. Kelly states that we need to accept the truth that we are wounded and broken. He says, "Acceptance of this truth allows us to make peace with the mess." What I realize is that the mess doesn't always go away. However, if we come to acknowledge and accept the mess, we can find peace and joy amid the mess and chaos during the storm.

As the Apostle Paul says, "Therefore, since we have been justified by faith, we have **peace** with God through our Lord Jesus Christ. Through him we have also obtained access by faith into this grace in which we stand, and we **rejoice** in **hope** of the glory of God. Not only that, but we **rejoice in our sufferings**, knowing that suffering produces **endurance**, and endurance produces **character**, and character produces **hope,** and hope does

---

[314]    Isaiah 48.10, ESV

not put us to shame, because God's love has been poured into our hearts through the Holy Spirit who has been given to us."[315]

Yes, in our suffering, during our messy life, the peace that passes all understanding is already well established by what Christ did for us on the cross. As a result, we can find joy and rejoice in the suffering. Even if the suffering never ends or the mess never gets better, God is with us, using everything to give us endurance, character, and hope.

Kelly writes these profound words, "It's okay that we are broken. It's only a problem if we subscribe to the false notion that we have to try to keep everyone and everything from being broken." There's a familiar saying going around these days that *it's okay not to be okay.* That's a hard lesson to learn. I constantly fall into the trap that *it's not okay to not be okay.* I also fall into the deadly habit of trying to make everyone believe that I am okay when I'm not.

Perhaps I am straining at the oars of *outward appearances.* That is an entirely different chapter I could add to this book in the future. I also fall into the unhealthy behavior of keeping others from being broken or fixing them when only God can give them what they need. *Ok, there's another chapter I could add here about how trying to fix or rescue others can keep us* straining at the oars. By trying to rescue or heal someone, I may stop what God wants to do within them to develop the peace, joy, endurance, character, and hope only he can give. My need to make sure everybody is okay may keep them from learning how to receive all God has already placed within them. God is ready and able and possibly still waiting to unleash all the resources from heaven into the depth of their soul. By interfering or messing with what God is doing, I may be keeping them from discovering

---

[315]  Romans 5.1-5, ESV

all the qualities of God that I wrote above and are available to them right now. I may be enabling them to continue the cycle they've been in for years.

Kelly goes on, "It's what we do with the mess that determines everything. You can ignore it, avoid it, deny it, blame others, shame yourself and exhaust yourself pretending your life isn't messy," or "you can realize that the mess serves a powerful purpose." Could it be that the purpose of our messy life, our suffering, is to find peace and joy in ways we never would otherwise? Could our suffering allow us to develop endurance and character to find hope beyond hope? Kelly says, "You don't have to have it all together. Nobody has it all together," and "the meaning of life isn't to solve the mess. That's not the goal." In our messy life, even amid our suffering, the goal is to draw closer to God and allow his glory to be revealed in the good, the bad, and the ugly.

Kelly then asks a question: "Can something that has been broken be put back together in a way that makes it more beautiful than ever before?" Isn't that what we all hope? Isn't that what we all want? It's not the story of Humpty Dumpty. It's about us, broken and flawed, and yet somehow we can be put back together even better than before. It's not about a makeover, it's a new creation, or a re-creation. What I came to realize is that after the resurrection, Jesus still had the scars from the nails that pierced his hands and feet, as well as from the sword that pierced his body. However, Jesus, in his resurrected state, was better than before. He was no longer constrained by human limitations. You may never be completely perfect or whole in this world. Kelly says, "Your imperfections are part of what makes you perfectly yourself." We are all broken and wounded. We all have scars. None of us is perfect. As Kelly says, "We believe that once something is broken it can never be as beautiful as before. But that's not true. Indeed it cannot be exactly the same as before, but that doesn't mean it cannot surpass its former self."

I do know that I am a masterpiece created by God. However, once that masterpiece becomes stained or torn, I would tend to believe that I am no longer as valuable as I once was. That is a life I have bought into my whole life. Kelly used an beautiful illustration that opened my eyes to the amazing truth about what it means to be new in Christ with my warts and all, as well as with my remaining scars and wounds.

Kelly shares about a beautiful Japanese art form called *Kintsugi*. As he says, "In our disposable culture, if we break a vase or a bowl, we throw it away and buy a new one." *Been there, done that.* If we throw away the broken vessel and replace it with a new one, he says, "We maintain the illusion that life is not messy." *It's like sweeping dirt under the rug or putting away all the junk from our desk into a drawer to hide it out of plain sight.* Here is where the art of *Kintsugi* gives a twist.

Kelly describes it as, "When a vase or bowl or cup is broken, artists gather up the broken pieces and glue them back together." *Again, been there, done that, but there's more.* "It is how they put them back together that is steeped in wisdom and beauty. They mix gold dust with the glue. They don't try to hide the cracks. They own them, honor them, and even accentuate them by making them golden. They celebrate the cracks as part of their story," and "they don't pretend the vase was never broken. They don't pretend that life is not messy. They don't pretend they are not broken. When we pretend to be someone other than who we are, our true self hides in fear and shame; the fear of being discovered and the shame of not being enough."

Then, Kelly says, "The most beautiful and surprising lesson the *Kintsugi* artform teaches us is this—we are each other's wounded healers. We each possess the gold dust needed to glue other people back together, making them more beautiful and loveable than ever." (You may want to read Henri Nouwen's *Wounded Healer.*) It's not that we can take away someone's pain, or can make them feel better, or that their mess will go away. The suffering, pain, wounds, and messy life that we experience in this world can and will be used by God to offer empathy and comfort to those God brings our way. "Blessed be the God and Father of our Lord Jesus Christ, the Father of mercies and God of all comfort, who comforts us in all our affliction, so that we may be able to comfort those who are in any affliction, with the comfort with which we ourselves are comforted by God. For as we share abundantly in Christ's sufferings, so through Christ we share abundantly in comfort too."[316]

My prayer is that whoever reads this book may taste the goodness of God and receive the riches of Christ. May the strength and comfort, joy, and peace of the Holy Spirit navigate you through the current and future storms of life that come from our living in a broken world. And that as you continue to rise out of the ashes with the comfort given to you by God, you might be an instrument, a vessel of hope and comfort for others.

And finally, as I have concluded many a worship service: "The LORD bless you and keep you; the LORD make his face shine on you and be gracious to you; the LORD turn his face toward you and give you peace."[317]

---

[316] 2 Corinthians 1.3-5, ESV
[317] Numbers 6.24-26, NIV

# REFERENCES

Scripture quotations and references marked *NIV* are taken from the New International Version. The Holy Bible, 1973, by *Zondervan Publishing House.*

Scripture quotations and references marked *AMP* are taken from the Amplified Bible. The Holy Bible, 1987, 2015, by *Zondervan Publishing House.*

Scripture quotations and references marked *ESV* are taken from the English Standard Version. The Holy Bible, 2001, by *Crossway,* a publishing ministry of *Good News Publishers.*

Scripture quotations and references marked HCS are taken from the Holman Christian Standard Bible, 1999, by *Holman Bible Publishers.* Scripture quotations and references marked *KJV* are taken from the King James Version. The Holy Bible, 1611, *Public Domain.*

Scripture quotations and references marked *NLT* are taken from the New Living Translation. *Holy Bible,* 1996, 2004, 2015 by Tyndale House Foundation.

Scripture quotations and references marked *MSG* are taken from The Message, 1993, 2002, 2018 by Eugene Peterson.

The following books are recommended for you to read as follows:

Arterburn, S (2011), 'Healing is a Choice', *Thomas Nelson.*

Barton, RH (2006), 'Sacred Rhythms: Arranging Our Lives for Spiritual Transformation', *IVP Books*

Bevere, J (2019) 'God, Where are You?', *Messenger International.*

Bonhoeffer, D (1995), 'The Cost of Discipleship', *Touchstone.*

Chambers, JO (2019), 'The Power of Transforming Prayer', *Our Daily Bread Publishing.*

Cloud, Dr H (2011), 'Necessary Endings', *Harper Business.*

Crabb, L (1997), 'Understanding Who You Are', *NavPress.*

Ferguson, S (2016), 'Devoted to God', *The Banner of Truth Trust.*

Grenny, J (2021), 'Crucial Conversations: Tools for Talking When Stakes are High', (3rd Edition), *McGraw Hill.*

Idleman, K (2014), 'AHA: The Good Moment that Changes Everything', *David C. Cook.*

Johnson, B (2017), 'Encountering the Goodness of God: 90 Daily Devotions', *Destiny Image.*

Kelly, M (2021), 'Life is Messy', *Blue Sparrow.*

Maxwell, J (2019), *Creating Position Change in* 'Developing the Leader Within You', *Harper Collins Leadership.*

Nouwen, H (1979), 'The Wounded Healer: Ministry in Contemporary Society', *Doubleday Image.*

Powell, K, and Griffin, B (2021), '3 Questions That Change Every Teenager', *Baker Books.*

Spurgeon, CH (2018), 'Morning and Evening: The Classic Daily Devotional', *Barbour Books.*

Stone, D (2010), 'Difficult Conversations: How to Discuss What Matters Most', *Penguin Books.*

Tozer, AW (1977) 'The Pursuit of God', *Tyndale House Publishers.*

Walling, TB (2015), 'Stuck: Navigating Life and Leadership Transitions', *CreateSpace Independent Publishing Platform.*

# REFERENCES

Willard, D (2012), 'Renovation of the Heart: Anniversary Edition', *NavPress*.

The following websites referenced in this book are as follows:

Facebook, https://www.facebook.com/.

Google, https://www.google.com.

Mayo Clinic—Mayo Clinic, 'Narcissistic personality disorder—Symptoms and causes—Mayo Clinic', https://www.mayoclinic.org/diseases-conditions/narcissistic-personality-disorder/symptoms-causes/syc-20366662, accessed 04/22/2022.

Quora, https://www.quora.com/What-are-the-common-characteristics-of-white-knight-narcissists, accessed 4/22/2022.

YouTube, https://www.youtube.com/.